The Santa Fe Trail
NEW PERSPECTIVES

**The Santa Fe Trail:
New Perspectives**
is a special issue of *Essays and Monographs in Colorado History* consisting of papers from the Santa Fe Trail Symposium, held in Trinidad, Colorado, from September 12 to 14, 1986. The symposium, sponsored by the Colorado Historical Society, was made possible through the generous support of the Colorado Endowment for the Humanities, Trinidad State Junior College, the Trinidad Historical Society, and the American Association of University Women.

COLORADO
HISTORICAL
SOCIETY

University Press of Colorado

Adapted from a map drawn by Frank A. Cooper

Published by the University Press of Colorado
P.O. Box 849
Niwot, Colorado 80544

All rights reserved.

Copyright © 1992 by the University Press of Colorado
Copyright © 1987 by the State Historical Society of Colorado

Cover illustration by Carrie Arnold.

The University Press of Colorado is a cooperative publishing enterprise supported, in part, by Adams State College, Colorado State University, Fort Lewis College, Mesa State College, Metropolitan State College of Denver, University of Colorado, University of Northern Colorado, University of Southern Colorado, and Western State College.

ISBN 0-87081-278-5

The paper used in this publication meets the minimum requirements of the American National Standard for Information Sciences—Permanence of Paper for Printed Library Materials. ANSI Z39.48–1984
∞

CONTENTS

Marc Simmons
The Poetry of the
Santa Fe Trail   1

David Lavender
Bent's Fort: Outpost of
Manifest Destiny   11

Sandra L. Myres
Women on the
Santa Fe Trail   27

Barton H. Barbour
James Ross Larkin:
A Well-Heeled Health
Seeker on the Santa Fe
Trail, 1856–57   47

Janet Lecompte
The Mountain Branch:
Raton Pass and Sangre de
Cristo Pass   55

Daniel D. Muldoon
Trappers and the Trail:
The Santa Fe Trail from
the Trapper's Perspective   67

David A. Sandoval
Who Is Riding the Burro Now?
A Bibliographical Critique of
Scholarship on the New
Mexican Trader   75

David Dary
Storied Silver, Fabled Gold:
Buried Treasure Legends
along the Santa Fe Trail   93

Jack D. Rittenhouse
The Literature of the
Santa Fe Trail: An
Introduction and Guide for
the New Traveler   109

Index   117

ESSAY ONE

Marc Simmons

The Poetry of the Santa Fe Trail

About the author
A national authority on the Santa Fe Trail and past-president of the Santa Fe Trail Council, Marc Simmons has written thirty books on the history of the American Southwest and on the Spanish borderlands. A popular lecturer and columnist as well as a scholar, Simmons received his M.A. degree and Ph.D. in history from the University of New Mexico. His most recent book is *The Last Conquistador: Juan de Onate and the Settling of the Far Southwest.*

Essays and Monographs

SOMEONE ONCE SAID that there is poetry in the story of old trails—in their history, in the country through which they passed, and in the lives and adventures of people who traveled them. If true, that would help explain why so many persons who have come in contact with the historic Santa Fe Trail have chosen to write poems about it. Their ranks include the likes of Sharlot Hall, Arizona's poet laureate; western novelist Eugene Manlove Rhodes; New Mexico's renowned cowboy poet S. Omar Barker; and even the distinguished American writer Vachel Lindsay.

The majority of the verse about the Santa Fe Trail, however, has been turned out by rank amateurs, by individuals who became caught up in the spirit of the trail. In its drama, its color, romance, tragedy, and humor they found a fit subject for creative effort. The quality of the poems ranges from artfully crafted gems to pure doggerel, but all of it can be described as sincere in sentiment. Of the quantity, no one can say with certainty, except that scores of trail poems are known, and many more may exist, as yet undiscovered.

The span of years the Santa Fe Trail was in existence (1821–1880) coincided with the "Age of Poetry," a time in the nineteenth century when verse filled the columns of newspapers and magazines, and new books of poems were announced almost daily by publishers. Great national events such as the Mexican War and the Civil War, as well as individual adventures like a crossing of the western prairies in a covered wagon, elicited a great outpouring of popular poetry. All were encouraged to join in its writing, and many accepted the invitation and did.

The earliest poem, so far known, that deals with the Santa Fe Trail was published in the *Missouri Intelligencer* on November 6, 1829. According to an editorial note, it represented a eulogy to the memory of a young merchant, Sammuel Craig Lamme, "who fell lately in an attack made by a party of Indians on his caravan, while on the prairie trace between Missouri and Santa Fe."[1] It seems that Lamme with two companions left the wagon train to scout ahead soon after crossing the Arkansas River in western Kansas on the Cimarron Cutoff. They were shortly set upon by Kiowas. In fleeing, Lamme fell behind because he was riding a mule while the others had horses. He was overtaken, killed, and scalped.

The first verse of the poem to this young man reads:

No sculptured marble marks the grave,
Where your remains, brave youth, are laid;
Nor drooping willows, pensive weave,
Around the spot, their humble shade.

It is a typical sentimental poem of the day, worth recalling only because it may, indeed, have been the first dealing with the subject of the trail.

In the decade that followed, the 1830s, two young men traveled to Santa Fe, both of whom wrote numbers of poems derived from their experiences. They were Albert Pike and Matt Field. Their poetry and other writings have been recently reprinted, but the poems are only of antiquarian interest, having no value as either literature or history.[2]

Over the years poems of the trail flowed forth in a steady stream. Some of them were about famous places along the route, like Independence, Council Grove, and Santa Fe. Others were written to commemorate notable incidents. For example, an English nobleman, Lord Frederick Haxby, happened to be at Fort Dodge in 1868 when four troopers, who had been carrying the mail to Fort Larned, were brought in wounded. They had been surrounded at Little Coon Creek and for hours fought off large numbers of attacking Indians. His Lordship was so impressed by their tale of heroism that in their honor he composed "The Ballad of Little Coon Creek." It was widely printed in newspapers, both in America and Great Britain. In fact, the ballad's popularity may have contributed to the four soldiers later being awarded the Congressional Medal of Honor.[3]

Another poem, this one about tragedy rather than heroism, was written to tell of the death of a young nun, Sister Mary Alphonsa, who perished in a well-known incident of 1867 while crossing the plains to New Mexico in the company of Bishop John B. Lamy. Above the Arkansas Crossing in Kansas, the wagon caravan to which the bishop's party was attached suffered a furious assault by several hundred Comanches.

After the enemy had been repulsed, the bishop wrote in his journal: "The youngest sister of Loretto [Mary Alphonsa] died, on the 24th of July, from fright, as I considered it, caused by the attack of the savages. She was eighteen years of age, well educated, and a model of virtue." Actually, the good sister had been suffering from cholera, but the terror occasioned by the noise of battle may have pushed her over the edge.

Afterward, a Catholic poet, Eleanor Donnelly, wrote about the sister's death in a poem that came to be loved by every Lorettine and familiar to the pupils in their schools, including the one that existed, until recently, in Santa Fe. The opening verse begins:

> They made her a grave where the tall grasses wave,
>   'Neath the blue of the western sky,
> And they laid her to sleep where the wild waves sweep,
>   Through the bending reeds that sigh.
> With a swelling heart they were forced to part
>   A link from that sacred chain,
> And though lovely and bright, it was laid at night,
>   'neath the sods on the Western plain.[4]

There exists a curious aftermath to the episode. Somehow word was carried from the plains that the bishop's train had been overcome by the Comanches. Papers in the East and in Europe carried stories proclaiming that the bishop with his priests and nuns had been killed and mutilated. Weeks later, when Lamy and his party arrived at the small settlement of Trinidad, at the foot of Raton Pass, they were astonished to read the lurid tale of their massacre in an old issue of the *Denver Gazette* and to hear that the local priest had sung a Requiem Mass for their souls.[5]

Preserving memory of events through verse seems to have been inborn in many pioneer Americans. Take an instance recorded by Senator James R. Doolittle, who headed a commission that traveled the Santa Fe Trail in 1865 to investigate Indian affairs following the Sand Creek Massacre. As the senator's party arrived at the summit of Raton Pass, he wrote: "When at length we reached the line of New Mexico many a shout and cheer went up with an occasional apostrophe—now in prose and now in rhyme—now to the enormous territories we had just traveled through and now to the greater one we were just entering."[6] In other words, as he tells us, someone authored a poem to mark the passage of the company into a new land.

The practice of honoring the Santa Fe Trail through poems continued well into the twentieth century, long after the trail had closed. Numbers of them were published in the Atchison, Topeka & Santa Fe company periodical called the *Santa Fe Trail Magazine*. An example that appeared in a 1913 issue is entitled "The Famous Old Trail" by Iona Cahill. The first verse goes:

> From Missouri's turbid stream
> To the old post, Santa Fe,
> In a long unbroken sea,
>   Runs a scarred and rutted way,
> Ling'ring 'round which many a tale
> Lives to mark the famous trail.[7]

While there is nothing remarkable in a literary way about this and similar poems, they do represent an interesting expression of nostalgia that many writers have felt toward the old road to Santa Fe. That nostalgia, together with an air of mystery, emerges in these lines penned by Santa Fe poet Arthur Chapman in the 1920s.

> And when the night has drawn its veil
> The teams plod, span on span,
> And one sees o'er the long dead trail
> A ghostly caravan.[8]

One of the best known poems of the trail, composed by James Grafton Rogers, was called simply "The Santa Fe Trail." Its popularity stems from the fact that it was set to music and has been recorded on several occasions. It opens with the familiar lines:

> "Say, pard! have ye sighted a schooner,
>   A hittin' the Santa Fe Trail?
> They made it here Monday or sooner
>   With a water keg roped on the tail,
> With daddy and ma on the mule seat,
>   And somewhere around on the way,
> A tow-headed girl on a pony,
>   A-jinglin' for old Santa Fe—
>   A-jinglin' for old Santa Fe."[9]

Here, as in the other examples given, one senses that adventure, excitement, and romance have colored the memory of the trail and cast a mythic glow over its history.

Even the most casual reading into America's past will suggest that moving west or southwest by covered wagon was an experience filled with danger, hardship, and discomfort. Still, the evidence found in contemporary diaries and journals and in recollections set down later would indicate that many of the participants remembered their journey to Santa Fe as an exhilarating time in their lives.

Marian Sloan Russell, who first went to New Mexico as a child in the 1850s, wrote, when she was in her nineties living in the Stonewall Valley of Colorado, that "my life as I look back seems to have been lived best in those days on the trail." And she added: "There have been many things that I have striven to forget, but not those journeys over the old trail. The lure it held for us! Seems the folks who made those trips in covered wagons never forgot them."[10] While she did not render her feelings in verse, she did speak in poetic terms.

The Santa Fe Trail, of course, was not traveled by pure romantics, but rather in the main by hard-headed businessmen—solid Yankee merchants out of Missouri who were willing to risk life and fortune in a bold bid to transport salable merchandise across an Indian-infested and storm-tossed prairie ocean in hopes of realizing a profit in Mexico's provincial capital of Santa Fe. But though engagement in commerce was their primary motive, they were not immune to the exotic lure of the trail, as Marian Russell would later describe it.

Most of the rough-edged Missouri traders had never been out of their own country. To them, distant New Mexico with its different language, customs, architecture, and natural scenery exerted a special appeal quite apart from its attraction as a marketplace. To embark upon a summer season of trading in Santa Fe and share the comradeship of other men similarly engaged, in a dangerous crossing of the plains, provided an opportunity for adventure that many were quick to seize. The theater of their activity was so vast, the action so memorable, and the backdrop of landscape so picturesque that it is scarcely surprising that writers should attempt to celebrate it all in poetry.

The meaning of the shining vision of the far Southwest is caught in a single line of a poem dating from the early 1850s. The last verse goes:

"Then hold your horses, Billy,
   Just hold them for a day;
I've crossed the River Jordan,
   And am bound for Santa Fe."[11]

The key line is the third one, with its reference to crossing the River Jordan. Beyond that river lay the Promised Land, in this case New Mexico. And at the end of the trail awaited the New Jerusalem, or Santa Fe, with its sunlit plaza where merchants could hope to find their pot of gold at rainbow's end. Here was the stuff of poetry, indeed!

So much so that more than one hundred years later, the bards are still at work. In 1982 Welborn Hope, recognized as Oklahoma's "tramp poet," published his 176-page *The Prairie Ocean: An Epic Poem of the Santa Fe Trail*. In it he caught the dreamlike quality of a caravan's arrival in the Promised Land, as witnessed in these lines:

> Through Pecos village soon we passed, and saw
> The far blue ranges of Sandia—now
> A vast plateau we traveled, taking us
> Due north to Santa Fe, our Rainbow's End.
> We saw the far-off wave-like mountains rise
> In billows as if beaten up by wind—
> Up from the Prairie Ocean's body heaved
> Eight hundred miles by an enormous gale.
> Sweet Santa Fe! Before us in late sun,
> A sweep of low carnelian-colored hills
> Ran red like muscled arms into the town.[12]

The Santa Fe Trail thus remains the domain of the poet as well as the scholar. As long as some of its history is still untold and some of its poetic images are yet to be formed in words, the long old trail will continue to attract writers in search of their own literary Promised Land.

Indeed, the mere recitation of familiar names along the route of the Santa Fe Trail is a kind of poem of its own, one that was undoubtedly repeated in a variety of ways by seasoned travelers of the trail to their children and grandchildren. One of these renditions may have gone like this:

THE ROUTE
OF THE SANTA FE TRAIL

> It starts in Old Franklin, Missouri,
> Crosses the Big Muddy to Arrow Rock,
> Then west to Malta Bend, Lexington,
> And Fort Osage.

Beyond the fort, wagons loaded up at
Wayne City Landing, Independence,
    Westport and Westport Landing
...and crossed into Kansas at the
Whiskey village of New Santa Fe.

Over the prairies, tire tracks ran to
Lone Elm, the Oregon Trail Junction,
Black Jack, Palmyra, Brooklyn,
Flag Spring, 110 Mile Creek,
Switzler's Bridge, Dragoon Crossing
(Where Private Hunt is buried),
Havanna Stage Station, and Wilmington,
Thence by Big John Spring to the great
Campground at Council Grove on
The Neosho River.

Past the Grove the land opened wide by
Elm Creek to Diamond Spring, Lost Spring,
Cottonwood Crossing, and the web of
The Turkey Creeks.
Then westward to Little Arkansas Crossing,
Jarvis Creek, Cow Creek Station,
Plum Buttes, Fort Zarah and the Great Bend,
To famed Pawnee Rock where travelers
    carved their names;
To Ash Creek and Fort Larned on the
    Pawnee Fork,
Thence up the Arkansas to Forts Dodge
    and Atkinson,
And a place on the river known as
    the Caches.

Until the caravans came to a fork
    in the trail
Where wagonmasters had to chose
Between the shorter, dry Cimarron Cutoff
Or the longer but well-watered Mountain Branch.

Following the dry route they
    braved the dreaded Jornada
To come at last to water at
    Wagon Bed Springs on the Cimarron.

Thirty miles beyond lay Middle Spring
    at Point of Rocks,
Then Willow Bar, Upper Spring,
    Cold Spring and Autograph Rock,

McNees Crossing and the Rabbit Ears,
    Alamo Creek, Mount Dora, and Round Mound.
And the far side of Whetstone Creek,
Scouts kept sharp eye at another
    Point of Rocks,
At the Rock Crossing of the Canadian
And Santa Clara Spring at Wagon Mound,
For hostile Apaches and Utes that lurked
    about.
Next stop: La Junta (above Fort Union) as the forks
    of the trail rejoined.
For those who chose the long way
    through western Kansas and Colorado,
The trail led up the Arkansas to Chouteau's
    Island, Pretty Encampment, and Big Timbers
To Bent's New Fort and Old Fort Lyon
And on to Boggsville and Bent's Old Fort
Where the trail pointed southwest
    from a river ford
And ascended Timpas Creek to Hole-in-the-Rock
    and Trinidad,
Where, by Fisher's Peak and Wootton's toll gate,
Raton Pass opened on New Mexico at Willow Spring.
From there by a rock-strewn plain
Travelers hurried past Vermejo Station,
Cimarron Town, Rayado, and after
Ocaté Crossing swung north of the
Turkey Mountains to Fort Union
And La Junta.
One trail again, the Santa Fe route
Struck Gallinas Creek at Las Vegas,
Swung through Kearny Gap,
Down to Tecolote and over the divide
    to San Miguel and San José
West of the Pecos.
From a campground at Kozlowski's Ranch
    and Pecos Mission ruins,
The trail climbed to the top of Glorieta Pass,
By way of Pigeon's Ranch
Then on to Cañoncito and Rock Corral Stage Station.
And at last wheel ruts made a circle on the old plaza
    at Santa Fe—having spun out 1,000 miles,
To trail's end.

Essays and Monographs

1
Both the editorial comment and the poem can be found in *Westport Historical Quarterly* 7(June 1971): 10–11.

2
David J. Weber, ed., *Albert Pike: Prose Sketches and Poems* (Albuquerque: Calvin Horn, 1967); and John E. Sunder, ed., *Matt Field on the Santa Fe Trail* (Norman: University of Oklahoma Press, 1960).

3
David K. Strate, *Sentinel to the Cimarron* (Dodge City: Cultural Heritage and Arts Center, 1970), 77–78.

4
The bishop's quote and the poem are found in Anna C. Minogue, *Loretto: Annals of the Century* (New York: America Press, 1912), 144–46.

5
Paul Horgan, *Lamy of Santa Fe* (New York: Farrar, Straus and Giroux, 1975), 343, 349.

6
"Notes and Documents," *New Mexico Historical Review* 26 (1951): 152.

7
Santa Fe Trail Magazine, September 1, 1913.

8
Quoted in Margaret Long, *The Santa Fe Trail* (Denver: W. H. Kistler, 1954), 3.

9
Katie Lee, *Ten Thousand Goddam Cattle* (Flagstaff: Northland Press, 1976), 221–22.

10
Marian Russell, *Land of Enchantment: Memoirs of Marian Russell along the Santa Fé Trail as Dictated to Mrs. Hal Russell* (Evanston, Ill.: Branding Iron Press, 1954), 71.

11
W. W. H. Davis, *El Gringo; or, New Mexico and Her People* (Santa Fe: Rydal Press, 1938), 4.

12
Welborn Hope, *The Prairie Ocean: An Epic Poem of the Santa Fe Trail* (Oklahoma City: Oklahoma Historical Society, 1982), 57.

ESSAY TWO

David Lavender

Bent's Fort
Outpost of Manifest Destiny

About the author
A prolific writer and historian, David Lavender is a recipient of two Guggenheim Fellowships and the author of over thirty books on the American West. Among these are *Bent's Fort* (1954), which remains a standard work on the subject, *Land of Giants* (1958), *The Fist in the Wilderness* (1964), *The Rockies* (1968), *The Southwest* (1980), and other books which together examine the broad patterns of western exploration, settlement, and development. His *Let Me Be Free: A Nez Pierce Tragedy* was published by Harper Collins in May 1992.

Essays and Monographs

IN ONE THOUSAND and seventy-eight days between the formal annexation of Texas on March 1, 1845, and the signing, on February 2, 1848, of the Treaty of Guadalupe Hidalgo, ending the war with Mexico, the United States added nearly 1.2 million square miles to its national domain. The vast sprawl of Texas, the American Southwest, the Oregon country south of the forty-ninth parallel—all were gobbled up during this single, extraordinary surge of expansionism. So, too, were many lives and landmarks. The Alamo, Chapultepec, Bent's Fort, the Bent brothers—destiny used them and destroyed them, just as it came very close to destroying the federal union it so radically enlarged.

Destiny. Manifest Destiny. Just what *are* we talking about? If we can sort out the strands and reach a definition, then perhaps we can see how the Bent tragedy fits into and illuminates, in its small way, some of the characteristics that marked the headlong growth of our nation.

Although the words *manifest* and *destiny* were not paired politically until 1845, the energies they came to represent were as old as the Pilgrims. "Go West, young men—and women—and find a better world": that faith ignited and sustained one of the greatest mass migrations in history. It brought the United States into being and sent Lewis and Clark to the Pacific on a trip whose impact has never left the American imagination. That faith also led Silas Bent, the father of the four fort-building Bent brothers, to move from Massachusetts to Ohio and then to Missouri, where he became principal deputy surveyor in charge of recently founded Louisiana Territory. Other human atoms in the continuing migration were the St. Vrains, one-time nobles in France. Ruined by the Revolution there, they too eventually reached Missouri.[1]

The magnet kept tugging at some of the next generation of Bents and St. Vrains. After a variety of separate, sometimes dangerous, and seldom profitable adventures in the Rocky Mountains and what is now the Southwest, Charles and William Bent—Charles nine years the elder—and Ceran St. Vrain came together as partners in the Santa Fe trade. An outgrowth of that commercial union, of course, was the adobe fort on the Mountain Branch of the Santa Fe Trail.

The building of the post was occasioned by a significant shift in the pattern of the fur trade. Initially the quest had been for beaver. Initially, too, Indians had been the chief hunters, and the pelts they harvested were bartered from them at conveniently located trading houses. As the fur frontier reached the upper Missouri, the Rockies, and the mountainous parts of the Southwest, however, whites turned out to be more proficient trappers than the horse Indians were. Most fixed posts lost their reason for being. Fur brigades roamed far and wide. The trappers in the north came together at annual summer rendezvous to turn in their catches, squander their pay, and gather supplies for the following winter.[2]

Farther south, the rendezvous did not take hold, partly because the Mexican government would not have allowed so blatant an intrusion by foreign fur companies. Trappers there worked in smaller parties. They sold their pelts and bought their supplies from merchants who maintained small, odorous general department stores in Taos, somewhat removed from the scrutiny of the officials in Santa Fe. The merchants also sold goods to local inhabitants, and if unsold items accumulated, they were carted off as far, sometimes, as Chihuahua, Durango, or even California—goals, also, of storekeepers in Santa Fe. It was in Taos that the original firm of Bent & St. Vrain took shape in 1829.[3]

By the early 1830s, overhunting had reduced the availability of beaver throughout the West. Scarcity, however, did not raise prices, for beaver hats were losing their popularity. Concurrently, more and more easterners were using buffalo robes as winter lap robes in their sleighs and as throw rugs in front of their fireplaces. As a result, the price of buffalo hides, along with that of the choice edible parts of the huge beasts, began edging up. Quick to note this, the principal fur companies adapted their procedures to take advantage of the change.

In a sense, this was a step backward. Indians again became the principal hunters—preparing buffalo robes was a grubby work whites gladly left to red women they called squaws—and bartering for the pelts reinstituted fixed trading posts. Considerations of safety were also involved. The Plains Indians might not trap beaver, but they had made a life ritual out of hunting buffalo and would have fiercely resisted attempts by whites to muscle in commercially on their principal natural resource.

Though the halcyon days of trapping were over by the early 1830s, the industry was by no means dead. Accordingly the firm of Bent & St. Vrain—soon to become Bent, St. Vrain & Company with the addition of brothers Robert and George Bent and Marcellin St.

Vrain—wanted to locate its new post where it could be reached both by the mountain men who roamed the southern Rockies and the Cheyenne, Arapaho, Ute, Kiowa, and Comanche, who crisscrossed the southern High Plains. The new fort, they told each other, should also be close to the company stores at Taos, yet not on Mexican soil, where it would be subject to arbitrary taxation and interference by New Mexico's unpredictable governors. The last-named consideration necessitated a location north of the Arkansas River, which in those days served as part of the boundary between the United States and Mexico.

The task of locating and building the post fell to William Bent. Just how calculated his early experiments were cannot be said. Probably trial and error as well as pressure from competitor John Gantt, who built an adobe post near the site of present-day Pueblo, guided him as much as logic did. In any event he did construct, in 1833 or so, a wooden stockade close to the junction of Fountain Creek and the Arkansas River, near Gantt's establishment. It seems likely, too, that Bent had another stockade at the Big Timbers, an extensive grove of stately cottonwoods down river toward today's Lamar, Colorado. Neither location suited demands as they were perceived at the time, and in the end he settled on a riverbank site roughly nine miles above Purgatory Creek and close to the place where the Mountain Branch of the Santa Fe Trail swerved southwest up Timpas Creek toward Raton Pass.[4]

The adobe castle that resulted was powerful for the era. Walls fourteen feet high, with eighteen-foot bastions at opposite corners, formed a rectangle 130 feet wide by 180 feet long. There was a wedge-shaped corral along one side, wagon sheds and a wagon yard to the rear. Living and work rooms surrounded an inner plaza. Their roofs could be used for promenades, and the outer walls, which rose about four feet higher than the roofs, could be used as parapets in case of attack. Eventually a billiard room and bar and a few dwelling rooms would be added to form a partial second story. In the center of the plaza, as prominent as a statue or an identifying fountain, was a wooden press for compacting buffalo hides into bales that could be readily loaded into freight wagons.[5] Adventures in commerce were definitely and always a primary motive behind the western urge—or to put it another way, of imperialism on the home front.

The fort was probably built in 1834, though Sam Arnold has argued cogently that it did not come into full use until 1835.[6] By that time, nearby competition had been stifled, and soon (probably 1837) the firm had located a branch store, eventually named Fort St. Vrain, on the South Platte River, within reach of the Oregon Trail.

Significantly for our discussion, the 1830s was also the decade when the first missionaries, precursors of settlement, faced westward along the trail that led past Fort Laramie (built in 1834) and over South Pass into the Oregon country. During that same decade the Choctaws, Creeks, Chickasaws, Cherokees, and Seminoles were pressured into ceding their lands to the United States and moving along the notorious Trail of Tears into Indian country (present Oklahoma), out of the way of southern cotton planters. It was the decade when rebellious Texans won independence from Mexico. President Andrew Jackson, looking westward toward what he called, in the best public relations fashion, "new areas of freedom," sent William Slacum off by ship to spy on Oregon and California. The latter province he offered to buy, along with Texas, from Mexico.[7] Though Mexico turned him down, destiny was clearly gathering headway.

Unfortunately for Jacksonian Democrats, the Panic of 1837 interrupted the march. Whigs took over the government in 1840, installing William Henry Harrison as president. To small avail. A month after the nomination, Harrison died of pneumonia, and John Tyler, who was really a Democrat in Whig clothing (he had left the Democratic party because he could not stomach Jackson), stepped into the White House.

Because Tyler was neither fish nor fowl, the Whigs declined to nominate him in 1844 and instead substituted, as their presidential candidate, Henry Clay. The Democrats responded with James Knox Polk, who boldly chose to campaign on an expansionist platform of *re*annexing Texas and *re*occupying Oregon. The naked imperialism just barely worked. Polk's margin in a popular vote of roughly 2.6 million was a thin 37,000—less than one tenth of one percent of the total! A scant shift of a few thousand votes in New York, which commanded a large block of electoral votes, and in Michigan would have defeated him. Because of New York, however, the electoral college vote looked respectable—170 to 105.[8] Of greater importance, several war-hawk Democrats were sent to Congress. Reading the results as a mandate for expansion, the hybrid Tyler renewed efforts he had made earlier in his presidency to annex Texas. This time he succeeded by means of a joint congressional resolution. In spite of Mexico's strenuous objections, he signed the act on March 1, 1845, three days before Polk's inauguration.

Though Charles Bent seldom, if ever, voted in an American election—no polling places were near the scene of his activities—his sympathies were with the Whigs. After learning from Manuel Alvarez, the United States consul in Santa Fe, of Polk's election, he replied glumly that he wished the choice had been Clay. The Democratic victory, he wrote, was likely to stir up trouble between the United States and Mexico.[9]

He was familiar with the frontiers of both countries. When he was not on the trail to and from Missouri, supervising the progress of the company's wagonloads of pelts and merchandise, he lived in Taos. About 1835 he married a local beauty, Ignacia Jamarillo, but never took out Mexican citizenship. He was the self-appointed protector of Americans in northern New Mexico. He helped gain "drawback" rights for himself and his fellow merchants—a law that enabled a trader who had paid U.S. custom duties on the goods and afterwards paid additional Mexican duties on the same goods to obtain a refund. He protested discriminatory tariffs against American traders. On at least four occasions he railed at the Mexican authorities for not bringing the murderers of American citizens to justice, and he officiously did what the police neglected doing: he gathered up the victims' personal possessions for return to the nearest kin.[10] Though only five feet seven inches tall, he could be a mountain of belligerence. On being threatened with a suit by a Mexican national, he snorted contemptuously, "I had rather have the satisfaction of whiping [sic] a man that has wronged me than to have him punished ten times by the law."[11]

His bête noir was Padre Antonio José Martínez, parish priest of Taos and a leading member of the rich "big family" of northern New Mexico. Martínez has had a bad press in the United States, mostly because Willa Cather chose to make him the gross, treacherous, lustful antithesis of her hero, Jean LaTour (actually Archbishop Lamy) in her New Mexico novel *Death Comes for the Archbishop*. Charles Bent disliked Martínez fully as much as Cather did. In a letter to the consul, Alvarez, he accused Martínez of worshipping Bacchus more than any other god, of vanity, physical cowardice, and flagrant dishonesty—but not of sexual immorality, Cather's favorite denigration.[12]

Whatever the priest's personal foibles, he was a patriot and sought to improve the lot of his fellow citizens. He opened the first school in the area. His aim was to prepare likely young men for the priesthood, for there was a dire shortage of trained ecclesiastics in New Mexico—and, indeed, several of his students did become priests. In order to provide his pupils with books and catechisms, he bought the only printing press in New Mexico and turned out with his own hands the material he needed. He also used the press for a short while to print New Mexico's first newspaper, *El Crepúsculo de la Libertad* [The dawn of liberty].[13]

More to the point, Martíinez wrote and, on November 28, 1843, printed a ten-page pamphlet analyzing the ills of the department. He mailed copies to President Santa Anna and to New Mexico's most influential inhabitants. In the pamphlet, he leveled an accusing finger at American hide traders, by whom he clearly meant Bent, St. Vrain & Company. Those unscrupulous men, he charged, debauched the Indians with alcohol and thus persuaded them to kill so many buffalo cows that they were depriving themselves of their future livelihood. To obtain booty for whiskey, he went on, the Indians also preyed on the helpless ranchers of New Mexico.[14]

The accusation seemed substantiated early in 1846 when heavily armed Utes made off with several thousand head of livestock belonging to the "big family." The priest blamed Bent traders for arming the Indians, a charge Charles Bent vehemently denied. Shortly thereafter Bent found an additional cause for fury. An unruly Taos mob beat up his brother George and a companion, Francis Blair, of the influential Blair family of Missouri. During the fracas, the town justice, Martínez's brother Pasqual, looked on approvingly.[15]

The real sticklers, however, were the enormous land grants Governor Armijo began passing out in the early 1840s. He had two justifications. First, New Mexico's population was growing and demands for land could be met if energetic grantees undertook to colonize the vacant areas in the northern part of the territory. Second, the colonies, if established, would create a buffer against land-hungry Americans and, even more, against the rambunctious inhabitants of Texas, then an independent republic suspected of casting covetous eyes on New Mexico.

Because Charles Bent was not a citizen of Mexico, he could not legally obtain a land grant anywhere in that nation. Ceran St. Vrain and other former aliens could, however, for they had taken out citizenship papers. So could their prosperous Mexican acquaintances. Eight of these people applied for and were granted tentative title to more than seven million acres. Charles Bent was quietly given a sixth interest in two of the holdings.[16]

Discovering the illegality, Martínez reacted vigorously. He was not necessarily being altruistic. His relatives had also applied for a pair of huge grants in the north, and if all went through, real competition for suitable colonists would develop. So he fought hard against the grants in which Charles Bent was involved, but to no avail. Governor Armijo had also been quietly given a sixth interest in the same two massive properties, and after delays for the sake of appearances, the title was confirmed.[17]

Such is a sparse outline of Charles Bent's relations with the territory in which he had chosen to make his home. But how does this fit in with the broader picture of Manifest Destiny? By defining the term, perhaps we can tell.

The wedding of the words *manifest* and *destiny* did not occur until 1845. The matchmaker was John O'Sullivan, prolific writer and editor of several partisan journals. He first introduced the term to the public in the July-August issue of the *Democratic Review*. Why, he demanded rhetorically, did many Whigs and a few recalcitrant Democrats still complain about the annexation of Texas? Couldn't they see that other nations—he meant Britain and France—were meddling there in the hope of checking "the fulfillment of our manifest destiny to overspread the continent allotted by Providence for the free development of our yearly multiplying millions"?

Never one to let a good phrase lapse, O'Sullivan returned to the two words in the *New York Morning News* of December 27, 1845. The quarrel with Britain over title to Oregon was growing tense. Impatient with the legalistics of the diplomats, the journalist cried out, "Away, away with all these cobweb tissues of rights of discovery, exploration, settlement, continuity, etc. . . . Our claim to Oregon . . . is by the right of our manifest destiny to possess the whole of the continent which Providence has given us for the development of the great experiment of liberty and federated self-government."

This time the phrase caught on. Within a week Manifest Destiny was being hailed in Congress as "a new right in the law of nations." The power of suggestive language: American expansion was now seen as God-ordained and irresistible, hence blameless.[18]

Now to consider what all this actually meant. First, those lofty words about "the great experiment of liberty and federated self-government": they were not to be taken too literally, as Professor Thomas R. Hietala of Dartmouth College argues in chapter five, "Continentalism and the Color Line," in his book *Manifest Design*, published in 1985. White pioneers were the ones who were going to overspread the continent for the development of the great experiment. If nonwhite Mexicans or Indians or amalgamations of the two were too stubborn or too numerous to be absorbed, that was their hard luck. Away, away with them. They were not worthy of the gifts of liberty and self-government.[19]

Slandering your enemy is an old ploy, of course. Listen to Senator Edward Hannegan of Indiana. The Mexicans, he declared, were "utterly unfit for the blessings of liberty. . . . [T]hey cannot comprehend the distinction between regulated freedom, and that unbridled licentiousness which consults only the evil passions of the human heart."[20] Now listen to Charles Bent. "They are not fit to be free. . . . [E]very speses of vise in this country is a recomendation to public office. . . . The Mexican caracter is made up of stupidity, Obstanacy, Ignorance duplicity and vanity." (This strange screed, written as war approached, is still preserved among the Bent-Alvarez papers in the Read Collection at the Museum of New Mexico.[21] As far as I know it was never given public airing; Alvarez may have acted as a restraining force. Nevertheless, the document fits squarely with the racist traditions of Manifest Destiny.)

Let us turn back now to journalist O'Sullivan's initial definition of Manifest Destiny as "the free development of our yearly teeming millions." The awkward phrase "yearly teeming millions" apparently refers to a startling revelation made by the census of 1840. America's population was doubling every twenty-three years. It is part of Professor Hietala's thesis that anxious Democratic leaders, worrying over how to care for this relentless growth, deliberately designed the program that O'Sullivan labeled, in a flash of linguistic genius, Manifest Destiny.[22]

One part of their solution was the development of commercial outlets for both agricultural and manufactured products. The Orient was seen as the best potential market—after all, the far side of the Pacific had been a merchant's dream ever since 1785, the year that marked the return of the ship *Empress of China* to New York via

Cape Horn with a hold full of Far Eastern exotics. In 1845 Representative Caleb Cushing, member of a Massachusetts shipping family that already was trading in Hawaii and Oregon, managed to talk the reluctant Chinese rulers into a formal trading treaty.[23] Simultaneously Asa Whitney, a merchant who had long dealt with the Chinese, was advocating a transcontinental railroad that would eliminate the long, taxing journey around Cape Horn.

There were problems, to be sure. The nascent plans could not be truly successful unless America acquired ports on the Pacific. Puget Sound was one possibility; San Francisco Bay was another. The English, until eliminated by a surprising treaty completed early in 1846, were a barrier to the first. Mexico held the second. It was a loose hold, however, and could probably be broken by a combined land and naval assault. Though several hundred miles of the land route lay in Mexican territory, a fifth column of American traders, Bent, St. Vrain & Company included, was already firmly established at the trail's head. If war developed, the company and its adobe post on the Arkansas would inevitably play a role. In short, commercial Manifest Destiny was ready to march, via Bent's Fort.

Another worry awakened by the census of 1840 was the growth of industrial urbanization. True, cities produced goods for trade, but in the minds of many observers, they also brought about poverty, overcrowding, evil, and a tragic loss of self-reliance. The best safety valve for these ills, expansionists argued, was the maintenance of a strong agrarian society, as recommended years before by Thomas Jefferson. Skeptical Whigs pointed out that large tracts of undeveloped land were still available inside the country, so why stir up trouble by adventuring outside? Pointing to the census, Democrats retorted that the population explosion would soon devour those internal tracts. Meanwhile reports were coming in about bountiful fields not just in Texas but in Oregon and California as well.[24]

Less was said about New Mexico, yet it offered, as did Texas and California, a wondrous wedge, the land grant. A noisy, longtime booster of the West, William Gilpin, destined to be the first territorial governor of Colorado, later bragged that he had mentioned the opportunity to certain Santa Fe traders while traveling with Frémont's expedition of 1843–44. Soon New Mexico would fall into American hands, he predicted.[25] Was it not wise to prepare?

Other tales say Frémont himself made the suggestion. Perhaps so, though the Bents and Ceran St. Vrain had long been familiar with Spanish land grants in Missouri; St. Vrain's family had even owned one for a time. So their own knowledge could have prompted them to act with dispatch when land grants became available through Governor Armijo. Speculating on a growing nation's hunger for land—that, too, was a part of America's westering urge. By the early 1840s this rampant speculative urge had reached New Mexico.

Finally, of course, there were the inescapable factors of geography. Bent's Fort and Raton Pass lay athwart the southern route to California. That self-evident truth had led Stephen Watts Kearny and his dragoons to the Arkansas post after they had scouted the Oregon Trail as far as South Pass in 1845. What questions Kearny asked during his consultations with the Bents and St. Vrain were not recorded, but a guess that they involved matters of military logistics and New Mexican attitudes probably would not be wide of the mark.[26]

A few weeks after Kearny had departed, Lieutenant John Charles Frémont rode in with sixty heavily armed men. They were on their way to California, just to keep an eye on things. With Frémont was Lieutenant J. W. Abert, under orders to return to Missouri by way of the Texas Panhandle, making maps as he went. He also completed detailed drawings of Bent's Fort, presumably because the army might want information about the frontier bastion. The Bents, of course, were fully aware of what Abert was doing.[27]

The next summer Charles Bent and Ceran St. Vrain again conferred with Kearny, this time at Fort Leavenworth in the northeastern part of present-day Kansas. By then, disputes with Mexico over the southern boundary of Texas had brought about Polk's formal declaration of war. As part of a military strategy already laid down, Colonel Kearny, soon to be elevated to a general's rank, was struggling to put together an army capable of invading the Mexican northwest, currently our Southwest.

The tentacles of that army quickly embraced Bent, St. Vrain & Company. Seventeen hundred uniformed men and their supply columns, plus a heterogeneous mob of traders and their teamsters, came together in a chaotic rendezvous at the fort. There final plans for the invasion were completed. Because Polk cherished a hope that the troops could reach California before winter, Kearny wanted a peaceful conquest of New Mexico. To that end he issued proclamations promising to respect Mexican lives and property and bring a halt to the Indian raids that harassed the province. Emissaries were sent ahead to subvert Armijo if possible, and when the army began its advance, William Bent led the party of scouts that reconnoitered the way.[28]

Whether Armijo was bribed or whether he hoped to retain, after the war, his secret share in two of the land grants he had issued, or whether he simply lost his nerve, cannot be stated with firmness. In any event, he fled and the conquest was as peaceful, during its initial stages, as Polk and Kearny had desired.

Following the president's instruction, the general established a civil government with Charles Bent at its head. The lieutenant governor, Donaciano Vigil, was a relative of Charles's wife. Vigil also served as registrar of lands and would handle grant matters, even though he was a principal claimant, along with Ceran St. Vrain, to the four-million-acre Las Animas grant just south of the Arkansas River. Charles Beaubien, one of the territorial judges appointed by Kearny, claimed, together with Guadalupe Miranda, 1.7 million acres south of the Las Animas grant. Charles Bent and Manuel Armijo each held a sixth interest in those two grants. And the rest of Kearny's appointments were either friends or business associates of Bent's. Ironically, this list of officials and a new code of laws for running the government were printed on the press that belonged to Padre Antonio José Martínez.

Irony plagued the rest of the narrative. Territorial expansion, which Polk's anxious Democrats hoped would bind the Union together, actually exacerbated the differences over slavery and almost destroyed the federation. Charles Bent was killed during an uprising in Taos. Confirmation of the grant titles he so earnestly tried to protect created, during subsequent years, spectacular frauds and no little violence.

Epidemics of cholera introduced by the onrushing whites caused havoc among the Indians. That and their sense of what was following in the footsteps of the army led to outbreaks of war. William Gilpin, who led some of the punitive campaigns against the tribes, used Bent's Fort as one of his bases. The Indian trade declined. Seeing a more prosperous future in New Mexico, Ceran St. Vrain dissolved his partnership with William Bent.

In 1849 Bent's Fort was set afire and partly destroyed, whether by Indians or Bent himself cannot be said with assurance.[29] In any case, Bent moved downstream and built a new, smaller fort. There he became an Indian agent, handing out government doles to the once-proud people among whom he had found his first two wives. In time he sold this new fort to the army and moved to a stockade at the mouth of the Purgatory River. There he watched Chivington's troops march toward the Indian encampment at Sand Creek, where three of his mixed-blood children were staying with their mother's friends and relatives. A world split in that fashion could end only in dismay—and it did, in the horrors at Sand Creek and its aftermath, all of which bring to mind a slightly revised version of the old proverb: "Be careful what destiny you seek, because you are likely to get it."

Essays and Monographs

1
For the ancestry of the Bents and St. Vrain, see David Lavender, *Bent's Fort* (Garden City, N.Y.: Doubleday & Co., 1954), 18–23, 49–52, 376–78. Short sketches in LeRoy Hafen's ten-volume *The Mountain Men and the Fur Trade of the Far West* (Glendale, Calif.: The Arthur H. Clark Company, 1965–71) include Harold Dunham, "Charles Bent," 2:27–48, and "Ceran St. Vrain," 5:197–316. See also Samuel P. Arnold, "William Bent," 6:61–84.

2
The Rocky Mountain fur trade is well covered in Dale Morgan, *Jedediah Smith and the Opening of the West* (Indianapolis and New York: Bobbs-Merrill, 1953); Bernard DeVoto, *Across the Wide Missouri* (Boston: Houghton Mifflin, 1947); and Don Barry, *A Majority of Scoundrels* (New York: Harper & Brothers, 1961).

3
For the Southwest fur trade, see David J. Weber, *The Taos Trappers: The Fur Trade in the Far Southwest, 1540–1846* (Norman: University of Oklahoma Press, 1959) and Robert Glass Cleland, *This Reckless Breed of Men: The Trappers and Fur Traders of the Southwest* (New York: Knopf, 1950).

4
George Hyde gives an Indian version, its dates demonstrably wrong, of how the fort was located, in *A Life of George Bent, Written from His Letters*, ed. Savoie Lottinville (Norman: University of Oklahoma Press, 1968), 42–43, 59–60. See also Janet Lecompte, "Gantt's Fort and Bent's Picket Post," *The Colorado Magazine* 41 (Spring 1964) and Samuel P. Arnold, "William Bent," as in note 1 above.

5
J. W. Abert's detailed sketch of the fort appears in Hyde, *Life of George Bent*, 102ff.

6
Arnold, "William Bent."

7
John W. Caughey, *California: A Remarkable State's Life History* (Englewood Cliffs, N.J.: Prentice-Hall, 1970), 156–57.

8
Thomas A. Bailey, *The American Pageant*, 2 vols. (Lexington, Mass.: D.C. Heath & Co., 1971), 1:306.

9
Bent to Alvarez, January 24, 1845. Most of Bent's letters to Manuel Alvarez were published in the *New Mexico Historical Review* (hereafter *NMHR*) sporadically from 1954 to 1957. The originals (which I used when preparing *Bent's Fort*) are in the Read Collection, Museum of New Mexico, Santa Fe.

10
Dunham, "Charles Bent." Also Bent to Alvarez, April 23, 1843, in Harold Dunham, "Sidelights on Santa Fe Traders, 1839–1846," *Denver Westerners Brand Book*, vol. 6 (Denver: University of Denver Press, 1950), 276–77. Bent to Alvarez, December 1, 1840; March 2, 1846; April 26, 1846, in *NMHR*, 1954 *et seq.*

11
Bent to Alvarez, February 19, 1841, *NMHR* 29 (October 1954): 315.

12
Bent to Alvarez, January 30, 1841, ibid., 313–15.

13
For starters in the literature defending Martínez, see Pedro Sánchez, *Memories of Antonio José Martínez*, ed. Guadalupe Baca-Vaughn (Santa

Fe: Rydal Press, 1978); C. V. Romero, "Apologia of Presbyter Antonio J. [José] Martínez," *NMHR* 3 (October 1928): 325–46; E. K. Francis, "Padre Martínez: A New Mexican Myth," *NMHR* 31 (October 1956): 265–89; Ralph Vigil, "Willa Cather and Historical Reality," *NMHR* 50 (April 1975): 123–34.

14
William Keleher, *Turmoil in New Mexico, 1846–1868* (Santa Fe: Rydal Press, 1952), 66–70.

15
Bent to Alvarez, May 3, May 10, June 1, 1846, *NMHR* 31 (April 1956): 160ff.

16
Harold Dunham, "New Mexico Land Grants," *NMHR* 30 (January 1955): 1–22, and "Coloradans and the Maxwell Grant, *The Colorado Magazine* 32 (April 1955): 131–45.

17
Protesting the grants: Dunham, "New Mexico Land Grants"; Myra E. Jenkins, "Taos Pueblo and Its Neighbors," *NMHR* 41 (April 1966): 107; Louis Warner, *Archbishop Lamy* (Santa Fe, 1936), 78–79; Bent to Alvarez, March 2, 1846, April 19, 1846.

18
Julius Pratt, "The Origin of Manifest Destiny," *American Historical Review* 32 (July 1927): 795–98.

19
Thomas R. Hietala, *Manifest Design: Anxious Aggrandizement in Late Jacksonian America* (Ithaca, N.Y.: Cornell University Press, 1985), 152–60.

20
Ibid., 156–57.

21
Bent-Alvarez papers, date uncertain but probably in 1845.

22
Hietala, *Manifest Design, passim.* Note especially 110–11.

23
Ibid., 62, 198–201.

24
Ibid, Chapter 4, *passim.*

25
Dunham, "New Mexican Land Grants with Special Reference to the Title Papers of the Maxwell Grant," *NMHR* 30 (January 1955): 3–4.

26
Dwight L. Clarke, *Stephen Watts Kearny, Soldier of the West* (Norman: University of Oklahoma Press, 1961), 85–100

27
J. W. Abert, *Western America in 1846–47,* ed. John Galvin (San Francisco, 1966).

28
Clarke, *Stephen Watts Kearny,* 116–62. Other accounts of the war on the New Mexican front are too numerous to be listed here.

29
Lavender, *Bent's Fort,* 315–16, 413–14.

ESSAY THREE

Sandra L. Myres

Women on the Santa Fe Trail

About the author
A professor of history at the University of Texas at Arlington, Sandra L. Myres specializes in the history of the Spanish, Mexican, and American Southwest. She is the author or editor of a number of books and articles on western topics, including *Cavalry Wife: The Diary of Eveline M. Alexander, 1866–67* (1977), *Ho for California: Women's Overland Diaries from the Huntington Library* (1980), and *Westering Women and the Frontier Experience, 1800–1915* (1982). Active in a number of professional organizations, she is past president of Westerners International and currently vice president of the Western History Association.

Essays and Monographs

THE GREAT PERIOD of overland travel in the United States has always held a fascination for Americans. The number of books published on the subject perhaps more than rivals other favorite western topics, such as the Alamo and George Armstrong Custer, and probably approaches the huge outpouring on the various gold rushes to California, Colorado, Idaho, and Alaska.

Most of this extensive trail literature, however, deals with the overland emigrant routes—the Mormon Road to the valley of the Great Salt Lake, the Great Platte River Road and its major branches, the Oregon and the California trails, and the various southern overland routes through New Mexico, Arizona, and Old Mexico to the Pacific. The Santa Fe Trail, although it certainly has its aficionados and its share of books, articles, and pamphlets, is not as familiar to most Americans. Moreover, the Santa Fe Trail was different from other overland routes. The Santa Fe Trail, after all, was not primarily an emigrant road in the same sense as the other, more familiar trails. Rather it was primarily a commercial and military road that happened to attract some emigrants as well.

In some ways, Santa Fe Trail travelers shared the experiences of their contemporaries on the other great nineteenth-century routes—fear of Indian attack; danger from disease; frequent, and often fatal, accidents; occasional difficult terrain and ofttimes miserable weather. But because it was not primarily an emigrant route, the Santa Fe Trail was frequented not by families but by men, traveling alone or in the company of other men. Thus, when we begin to consider women on the Santa Fe Trail, we immediately run into a problem—there were not very many, at least not in comparison with the other trails. For example, Merrill Mattes's extensive bibliography in *The Great Platte River Road* (1969) listed sixty-seven published accounts by women on just one of the emigrant roads, and an almost equal number have been discovered and published since Mattes's book appeared. In contrast, a bibliography of women on the Santa Fe Trail compiled by Marc Simmons in 1985 contained only twenty entries.[1]

Moreover, until fairly recently most historians have not considered women a part of the frontier experience. Ever since Frederick Jackson Turner's famous essay on the American frontier appeared in 1893, Americans have read about the "Winning of the West" in a series of both popular and scholarly books and articles that captured the adventure and romance, as well as part of the reality, of the West but which dismissed women as "invisible, few in number, and not important to the process of taming a wilderness."[2] The historians' frontiers have been as devoid of women as the Great Plains were supposedly devoid of trees. Turner's pioneers were explorers, fur trappers, miners, ranchers, farmers—all of them male; and succeeding generations of western historians continued to interpret the westering movement as primarily a male enterprise in which women played a largely invisible and subordinate role. Women, after all, one wrote, "did not lead expeditions, command troops, build railroads, drive cattle, ride Pony Express, find gold, amass great wealth, get elected to high public office, rob stages, or lead lynch mobs"; and such activities were what really built the West. Indeed, as one historian wrote in 1974, "no one has ever questioned, let alone analyzed the masculinity of frontier society. Since it is as obvious as the sun in the daytime, the subject has not been discussed."[3]

Even when historians did acknowledge the presence of women on the western trails and on the frontiers, they often portrayed them in ethereal, mysterious terms, or presented a stereotypic picture as false as that of the Hollywood Indian. Thus, westering women were usually described as Dreary Drudges and Hapless Helpmates or as Gentle Tamers and Saints in Sunbonnets with an occasional Calamity Jane, Bandit Queen, or Fighting Feminist thrown in for good measure. Indian, Mexican, and black women rarely appeared in these descriptions of pioneer women, but when they did they, too, were presented in stereotypic fashion as abused squaws or Indian princesses, seductive señoritas or saintly señoras, kindly southern mammys or faithful family retainers.

Generally all westering women were seen as reluctant, and often repressed and frightened, pioneers wrenched from home and hearth and dragged off into the terrible West where they were condemned to a life of lonely terror among savage beasts and rapine Indians. Thus, Emerson Hough could write in 1921 of the "gaunt and sad-faced woman sitting on the front seat of the wagon, following her lord where he might lead, her face hidden in the same ragged sunbonnet which had crossed the Appalachians and the Missouri long before." Or we can turn to historian Everett Dick's 1966 statement that women probably were responsible for "much of the retreat from the frontier." So pervasive is this myth of women as reluctant pioneers that it has influenced even historians who know better. Thus Marc Simmons wrote in the introduction to his Santa Fe Trail bibliography about

> the disinclination of the majority of nineteenth century women to abandon family hearth and friends and go ajourneying toward the Pacific in pursuit of an elusive prosperity. Those who did, frequently at the insistence of husbands or father, faced the hazards and discomforts of trail life with uncommon fortitude, but few there were who would not have chosen to forego the experience.

Fortunately, Simmons's better judgment and historical sense intervened, and that statement has been substantially modified in the final verson.[4]

Most of these perceptions of western women were shaped by male writers who did not read what women themselves wrote about the West. Or, if they did read the many journals, letters, and reminiscences written by women, they chose to ignore them in favor of more dramatic legends and myths. But something of women's own views of the western experience and their role in the Great Adventure of the West can be determined from the many accounts written by women on the nineteenth-century frontiers. Contrary to what we once thought, a good deal of primary source material relating to women has survived, and it can tell us much about the reality of western women's lives if we simply let them speak for themselves.

Of all the women associated with the road to Santa Fe, we know the least about the Indian, Mexican-American, and black women who traveled along the trail or lived in close proximity to it. Because they left no written records, they are often overlooked in descriptions of the trail, its travelers, and its residents. But we can discover traces of their lives in government documents and reports; in court and church records; in the journals and diaries of the men of the time such as Josiah Gregg, Rufus B. Sage, and George Ruxton; and in the records of Anglo women who traveled along the trail and commented on the other women they saw there. We can also turn to material culture, archaeology, and anthropology to help us learn something of these women's way of life.

For example, we know from Anglo women's accounts that black women traveled along the trail, usually as cooks or personal maids.

We also know that a number of different Indian peoples lived along the trail or journeyed along or near it on hunting and trading expeditions, and most of the Anglo journalists commented extensively on the native peoples they encountered. Indian women, especially among the Plains people, have often been depicted as downtrodden, abused drudges, indeed little better than slaves; but it is obvious from the many anthropological studies as well as from the observations of travelers and residents of the trail that women filled a crucial role in Indian society and were honored and respected among their own people.

Among the sedentary, agricultural peoples such as the Pueblos, women did not work in the fields but rather were responsible for the home and domestic arrangements much as they were in Anglo society. Women generally built the homes and owned them as well. Pueblo women cared for the children, prepared and preserved foodstuffs, and supplemented the foods men grew with piñons, berries, and other wild plants which they gathered. The women also produced pottery storage vessels, water jars, and cooking utensils; and although men were the primary spinners and weavers, Pueblo women also exhibited skills with textiles and decorated the cloth with embroidery or painted designs and fashioned it into items of clothing. After the Spanish conquest, Pueblo women integrated Spanish material culture into traditional activities. They learned to prepare and preserve new foodstuffs, produced the various materials demanded by the Spaniards as tribute, and some supplemented the hard-pressed Pueblo economy by wage work as servants and seamstresses.[5]

Among seminomadic peoples like the Kaw, Pawnee, Osage, and Navajo, who had a mixed hunting and gathering economy supplemented by gardening, women were responsible for the garden plots and helped supplement the food supply by gathering various wild plants. As in more sedentary societies, women also had primary responsibility for food preparation and the making of clothing as well as child care. After the introduction of sheep, Navajo women became responsible for tending the herds the tribe acquired.[6]

Hunting and warfare were the foundation stones of the society of most of the Plains peoples such as the Comanches, Kiowas, and Apaches as well as the Cheyenne and Sioux who occasionally came down to the caravan track. Their womenfolk traveled with the various bands and extended families and, like other Indian women, had charge of the preparation of food, the making of clothing, and the domestic arrangements of the camps. Among many of the Plains tribes, women "had charge of the travois and cared for the dogs who pulled them and they made and maintained the tipis that served as family homes."[7]

Some of the Indian women married white trappers and traders who lived along the Santa Fe Trail. Janet Lecompte has written about several of these women, including two trappers' wives: Nancy, a "good-natured Piute" and Ka–wot, a Shoshone woman whom George Simpson described as "a marvelous, ill-favored member of the tribe." Ka–wot was also reputed to have a bad temper, and her trapper consort later left her for a Sioux woman he named Marguerita. Like Ka–wot, some of the trappers' wives were "dumped," as Lecompte phrased it, "when the trappers left the mountains and took up residence at trading posts." But other white-Indian alliances were more stable. For example, Charles Autobees's Arapaho woman, Sycamore, was his constant companion for twenty years, and the Shoshone sisters Susan Briggs and Sarah Ann Burroughs accompanied their husbands when they left New Mexico for California, as did Lancaster Lupton's Cheyenne wife. Sometimes white men took Indian wives for political purposes, which gave these women special position and status. As examples, Lecompte points to William Bent's successive marriages to chiefs' daughters in order to keep peace with the Cheyenne and to John Poisal's wife, Ma–hom, who was the sister of the Arapaho leader Left Hand.[8]

Despite some stable relationships, Indian women living with white men did not usually participate fully in the social life of the various Santa Fe Trail communities. This was not true, however, of the many Mexican-American women who lived in small villages or on the various ranchos along the trail. Many came from families that had resided in the area for centuries, while others were recent arrivals; but all of them, as Lecompte points out, typified the pioneer women of the frontier "just as truly and nobly in their *rebosos* as did the much better publicized covered-wagon heroines in their poke bonnets."[9]

Although one male observer scoffed at the *mexicanas* who, he said, could do just three things ("grind corn on a rock, make tortillas and dance"), it is clear from other descriptions and records that they did far more than that.[10] As Lecompte and others have clearly documented, "they washed clothes in the river using the root of the soapweed" and spread the clothes to dry on bushes. "They sprinkled and swept the floors of their rooms several times a day.... [T]hey ground corn and chili peppers used in tortillas and *atole*. They took care of the smaller domestic animals, kept fires going, whitewashed rooms and plastered walls, dried the meat their hunter-husbands brought back, planted and tended little gardens.... [and] made clothes for themselves and their children."[11]

Most of these hard-working, rural women belonged to the *peón* or poorer class of Mexican-American society. Other *mexicanas* came from the *rico* or upper class and lived lives of some ease and luxury with plenty of servants to do their work for them. Like their Indian sisters, women of both classes married Anglo trappers, traders, and merchants. George and Charles Bent, Ceran St. Vrain, George Simpson, Lucien Maxwell, and Kit Carson all had Mexican wives or mistresses. Although some of these unions were little more legalized or stable than those of Indian women living with white men, others, as Lecompte notes, were "both consecrated.... [and] surely made in heaven."[12]

Both Indian and Mexican-American women not only lived along the Santa Fe Trail but traveled on it as well. Unfortunately, since they left no written records, we know little about their trips or what they thought of life on the trail, but perseverance and further research should make it possible to document at least some of their journeys. For example, Marc Simmons was able to establish the trip of Dolores Perea, who accompanied her brother-in-law, Antonio José Chávez, on a buying trip to Missouri in 1843, and other *mexicanas* undoubtedly made similar trips.[13]

Fortunately for historians and others interested in the Santa Fe Trail, not all of the women are as difficult to trace as the Indians and *mexicanas*. Anglo women who traveled along the trail after 1846 left a number of written records which enable us to learn something of women's lives and activities on the trail and their reactions to the countryside through which they traveled and the people they encountered along the way.

Certainly the best known of the female trail journalists was Susan Shelby Magoffin, who accompanied her husband, Samuel, along the trail to Santa Fe in 1846. Susan was born near Danville, Kentucky, on July 30, 1827. Her family was wealthy and highly respected, and she was brought up in an atmosphere of ease and comfort. She was well educated, something of a romantic, and very much in love with Samuel, whom she married in 1845. Their trip to Santa Fe was, in part, "an extended honeymoon safari," and Mrs. Magoffin traveled in luxury. "In addition to a small tent house, a private carriage, books, and notions, her indulgent husband provided her with a maid, a driver, and at least two servant boys. Well she could explain at one point: 'It is the life of a wandering princess, mine.' "[14] Despite wealth and luxury, Susan Magoffin was an observant and perceptive woman and interested in all that went on around her. She had at least a working knowledge of Spanish, and fortunately for us, kept a 206-page diary of her western trip which she entitled "Travels in Mexico Commencing June, 1846. El Diario de Dona Susanita Magoffin." The diary remained in private hands until 1926 when Stella M. Drumm, librarian of the Missouri Historical Society, persuaded Susan's daughter to permit its publication. Since then, Magoffin's book has been reprinted several times and has come to rival Josiah Gregg's *Commerce of the Prairies* as one of the most popular as well as one of the most accurate and detailed descriptions of life and customs along the Santa Fe Trail.

Certainly the most prolific of the Anglo journalists were the army officers' wives who traveled along the trail after 1846. There are at least ten published accounts written by army wives, and others undoubtedly exist in manuscript form. Like Magoffin, the officers' wives were well educated; they were perceptive observers; and they offered comments and insights that give a vivid, detailed, and intimate view of life on the trail. Among the best known of their accounts are those of Lydia Spencer Lane, who made several trips along the trail both before and after the Civil War, and Marian Russell, who made "five round-trip crossings" before settling permanently in the "Land of Enchantment."[15]

Another army journalist, Eveline Alexander, traveled with her husband, Colonel Andrew Alexander, and the Third Cavalry through Indian Territory to Fort Union in 1866. From Fort Union the Alexanders followed the trail north to Trinidad and Fort Garland and then returned south to Forts Union, Bascom, and Sumner before leaving New Mexico in 1867.[16]

About the time the Alexanders were leaving New Mexico, Alice Blackwood Baldwin journeyed down the trail from Fort Harker, Kansas. She halted her trip briefly at Trinidad where her first child was born and then continued on via Fort Union to Fort Wingate where she rejoined her husband. Still another army wife, Frances Boyd, lived at army posts in Nevada, California, and Arizona before arriving at Fort Stanton, New Mexico, in 1870. The following year, Mrs. Boyd went to New York to await the birth of her second child and then returned to New Mexico along a portion of the trail in 1872.[17]

Another 1870s traveler, Frances Marie Antoinette Mack Roe, married West Point graduate Fayette Roe in 1871 and immediately started westward to join Fayette's regiment at Fort Lyon, Colorado, where Mrs. Roe's spritely account of their frontier life begins. The peripatetic Libby Custer did not actually live or travel directly on the trail, but her account of her life at Fort Riley, Kansas, gives a detailed description of the country and people on the eastern end of the road.[18] Other published accounts by army wives include those by Josephine McCrackin Clifford, Genevieve LaTourette, Anna Maria Morris, Mrs. Byron Sanford, and Ellen Williams.[19]

With the exception of Marian Russell and Ellen Williams, whose husband served with the Colorado Volunteers during the Civil War years, none of the army wives remained in the West, but other women travelers did. Emily Harwood and Anna McKee were both Protestant missionaries sent to New Mexico by eastern mission boards. Harwood went to New Mexico in 1869 with her husband, a Methodist preacher whose circuit included La Junta, Fort Union, Cimarron, Vermijo, and Red River. The Kelloggs established several schools in New Mexico for both Mexican and American boys and girls including the Boys Biblical and Industrial School of Albuquerque. McKee, a graduate of Lindenwood College in St. Charles, Missouri, was sent by the Presbyterian Board of Missions to teach at the mission school at Taos in 1884. Her letters to her family, held at the Colorado Historical Society, give a vivid account of life in that Santa Fe Trail community.[20] In addition, there are published accounts by several Roman Catholic missionaries, including Sister Kotska Gauthreaux, Mother Mary Magdalen Hayden, and Sister Blandina Segale as well as a manuscript account by Sister Mary Joanna Welch held in photocopy at the Denver Public Library.[21]

As Marc Simmons has pointed out, "probably the largest single category of women to be found on the Trail was composed of those who accompanied their menfolk in the rush to the Colorado goldfields in 1859."[22] Although these women, and later wives and families of potential settlers, were the most numerous of the female travelers, there are fewer published accounts of their activities than for the army wives and missionaries. Of those listed by Simmons in his bibliography, only one is a book-length account—Julia Archibald Holmes's *A Bloomer Girl on Pike's Peak, 1858*, published in 1949 by the Denver Public Library. The other accounts are shorter and include the memoirs of Mamie Bernard Aguirre, the memoirs of Flora Spiegelberg, and the diary of Ernestine Huning. One additional woman's account is that of Susan E. Wallace, who accompanied her husband, newly appointed New Mexico governor Lew Wallace, to Santa Fe in 1878 and published an account of her life in New Mexico in 1888.[23]

Now that we have met the ladies, what can they tell us about the Santa Fe Trail, its travelers, and its residents? First, all of the women commented, sometimes extensively, about the conditions of travel—their conveyances, provisions, camping arrangements, and even suitable trail dress. Some women, like Susan Magoffin, traveled in fairly comfortable vehicles and in comparative luxury with cooks, drivers, and other servants. For example, Anna Maria Morris recorded that "Dr. McDougal bought a beautiful carriage just before leaving Leavenworth which I am to have the use of and also of his Poney [sic] which is perfectly gentle." She also had several maids, including her cook, Louisa, and a "Sargeant [sic] Jones as driver & guide" as well as the occasional services of another female cook who worked for the adjutant. Ernestine Huning, traveling with a train of freight wagons to Albuquerque with her new husband, merchant Franz Huning, also had a black cook and "china dishes, camp chairs, and a table." "We have plenty of company," she recorded, "and we are always merry."[24]

The army wives, too, usually had plenty of camp help in the form of civilian servants or enlisted men detailed to assist the officers and their families. Army families usually traveled in ambulances pulled by mules or horses. The ambulance, a stout spring wagon equipped with leather-covered seats and covered with a canvas top, was a popular vehicle among army personnel; many officers owned one for their personal use as carriages and pleasure vehicles as well as to transport their families from one post to another. For example, Lydia Lane noted that her party "had quite a comfortable 'outfit' for a lieutenant and family, owning a pretty little ambulance and as fine a pair of large gray mules as one would wish to see."[25]

Ambulances came in either two- or four-wheeled models and were considered fairly comfortable, although on the march they were often crowded with household goods and personal belongings, as Eveline Alexander reported:

> I was seated in a high rocking chair which was fastened by cleats to the bottom of the ambulance. Under my chair was my tin washbowl and pitcher ... ; in front was a box of books ... lunch basket, Andrew's and my bags, shawls, tin cups, a canteen of milk, one of water, etc. etc. Hanging from the top of the ambulance were two leather pockets, one of them containing my revolver, the other a field glass; a looking glass; my sewing basket; and a lantern also swayed to and fro. Indeed I cannot begin to enumerate the various articles with which I was surrounded ... and before I had been underway two or three hours, my compassion was imposed upon to such an extent that I took in Flora, Sullivan's Newfoundland pup, and Fan [her husband's hunting dog] who were both so tired with the unusual journey that they were glad enough to lay quietly down in the bottom of the ambulance.[26]

Nor was Alexander the only woman who traveled with a menagerie. Many of the army officers and their wives had dogs and horses as well as a variety of other pets. Alice Baldwin shared her blankets with a house cat and a litter of kittens, and Ernestine Huning traveled with not only a dog, Nero, but with "ten canaries which [she] brought from St. Louis."[27]

Not everyone found their accommodations comfortable, however, or described them with Eveline Alexander's good humor. For example, Frances Roe reported that she traveled from Kit Carson, New Mexico, to Fort Lyon, Colorado, in "a funny looking stage coach called a 'jerky,' and a good name for it, too, for at times it seesawed back and forth and then sideways, in an awful breakneck way." Sister Mary Joanna Welsh also had few kind words for her conveyance, a mail coach, which she described as "a rusty, dusty looking affair with seating for four passengers." Unfortunately, there were five passengers including a priest and an army officer. "Father Raverday and the Captain occupied one seat," Sister Mary Joanna reported. "We three sisters had to accommodate ourselves the best we could to the space afforded us by the other [and] such a jolting we had never experienced . . . and fear of being dashed against our companion passengers on the other seat annoyed us not a little."[28]

In addition to carriages, ambulances, and stage and mail coaches, women also traveled along the trail in freight wagons, springboards, and buckboards as well as in the large ox-drawn wagons so familiar on the emigrant trails. By the 1870s at least a part of the journey could be made by train, and by 1876 the first sleeping cars had become available; but this did not necessarily improve the comfort of the journey, as Susan Wallace complained. She denounced the sleeping cars as a "chamber of torture" and reported—one suspects only partially in jest—that "the gay conductor... told us in an easy, off-hand manner [that] a man had been found dead in one of the top berths some weeks before. I only wondered [that] any who ventured there came out alive." Nor was poor Wallace's ordeal over when she reached Trinidad and "left the luxury of steam and came down to the territorial conveyance," a buckboard, which, like the sleeping cars, was "an instrument of torture deadly as was ever used in the days of Torquemada and had anything its equal been resorted to then there would have been few heretics."[29]

Whatever their mode of transportation, all of the women found reason to complain at one time or another about the condition of the road—or lack thereof—for as Sister Mary Joanna noted on her 1864 journey, in those days there was "no road of course." Even on the portion of the trail where there was a fairly level and even track, the dust churned up by the wagons, the gnats, flies, and especially the mosquitoes made travel less than pleasant. Even the normally vivacious and uncomplaining Susan Magoffin quailed before a relentless assault of mosquitoes encountered along the Little Arkansas River. "Millions upon millions" of the insects, she mourned, knocked against the carriage and *"reminded me of a hard rain. It was the equal to any of the plagues of Egypt. I lay almost in a perfect stupor,* [and] the heat and stings made me perfectly sick."[30]

Sometimes the travelers were frightened by violent storms that soaked their bedding and clothing and threatened to blow over their tents and turn over the wagons. Such storms often turned the roads into boggy quagmires which enveloped the wagon wheels, impeded progress, and caused great consternation, not to mention cussing, among the men detailed to free them. Other days, as Alice

Baldwin reported, "the Plains were nothing but a vast waste, hardly a weed even was to be seen, while the dust which arose from the moving column was stifling."[31] In other places the road was hilly and rocky and sometimes precipitous, as Lydia Lane recorded of her trip from Santa Fe to Cantonment Burgwin. "You may go to the foot of any mountain in your neighborhood," she wrote,

> start up at any point regardless of stones, holes, or other impediments and you will have an idea of 'the road' to Burgwin. ... The scenery was magnificent, but we could not enjoy it, owing to the roughness of the road. Did we allow our eyes to wander for a moment to the lofty mountains around us, we were forcibly reminded of the rocks and pitfalls in our path by a jerk or a wrench which dispelled our dreams and brought us rudely back to the immediate surroundings.[32]

Perhaps it was remarks such as these which led historians to decide that, given a choice, women would have chosen to "forego the experience" of overland travel, whether on the road to Santa Fe or along one of the emigrant routes to the Pacific. But one must bear in mind that men also complained just as bitterly, although sometimes not so eloquently, of similar travel conditions and that the women who did complain usually were ready to make the trip again when circumstances dictated that they do so. Indeed, some made later trips out of choice rather than necessity. Even Lane, who had complained so bitterly about the Santa Fe–Burgwin route, had no hesitancy in sending for her sister to join her, commenting that although "she might hear the road was bad, I knew she could have no conception of what it was like until she tried it, and then it would be too late to turn back."[33]

In addition to storms, wind, dust, and the poor condition of the road, there were other discomforts. Some days the travelers had to endure blistering heat and scorching sun, while at other times they faced bone-chilling cold and snow. In some places there was no wood or water, forcing the travelers to make a dry camp or journey long after dark in order to procure these necessary items. The women also found much of local fauna and flora disagreeable. In addition to the gnats, flies, and mosquitoes of which Magoffin complained, there were rattlesnakes, spiders, and venomous insects, while Alice Baldwin noted that "grasshoppers also were a scourge, and at times the air was filled with the pests."[34]

Nor was the plant life particularly appealing. Frances Boyd wrote that in all her travels, "I never met with anything else which gave me so much trouble as the cactus plant. ... In regions where nothing else could be prevailed upon to grow, that useful but disagreeable plant always throve; and the more dreary, parched and barren the soil, the more surely did the cactus flourish and expand its bayonet-armed leaves" which were dangerous to both man and beast. Anna Maria Morris voiced a similar complaint. "I have taken two walks today," she recorded, "but I do not think I shall attempt it again [T]he roads are too sandy and the whole earth in this country is covered with Cacti and a kind of palmetto as to render a walk anything but agreeable."[35]

Women who traveled with small children had additional cause for concern. Boyd noted that "if very young children were allowed to wander in the least, one could safely depend upon finding them in the vicinity of the dangerous cacti," and, indeed, her young daughter fell victim to the vicious plant. After two days of drenching rain, Lydia Lane and her family were forced to camp in a grove of cottonwood trees. "The ambulance was too small to lie down in," she wrote, "so we sat up and held the baby on our laps, turn about. Suddenly she gave one of those hoarse, croupy coughs, terrifying with the most comfortable surroundings; but it was distracting situated as we were with every wrap more than moist, and thirty miles from a doctor or house of any kind."[36]

Indeed, there was a good deal of illness on the road, much of it more serious than croup, and women were understandably concerned about the health of their children, husbands, and traveling companions. "My husband and Mrs. Franz are both sick," Ernestine Huning recorded, and that "is bad when we can do nothing for them." At times the women themselves fell ill. Susan Magoffin miscarried and lost her first child at Bent's Fort. Alice Baldwin was more fortunate in that her child lived, but giving birth in a strange place and without the services of a familiar doctor must have been a frightening experience for her.[37]

The women also worried about danger from hostile Indians, and although none of them was ever in serious peril herself, there were enough rumors and alarms and reminders to keep them in a state of some anxiety. Like women on the overland trails, the Santa Fe travelers recorded the sites of graves and the spots where Indian attacks reputedly had occurred.

In addition to all of these troubles, much of the journey was monotonous, boring, and tiring. "None of us had been attracted or interested in the dreary, wind-swept Plains or the inhospitable appearance of the country," Alice Baldwin wrote. "The days were all alike, monotonous and tedious, varied occasionally by the mules stampeding." Sister Mary Joanna reported that over much of their route there was "nothing but unattractive scenery," and most of the other women voiced similar sentiments.[38]

But women's accounts of trail travel were not one long, dreary dirge of danger and discomfort. They also recorded the pleasures of the journey and wrote of the beauties of the countryside, the "cool delicious air of the mountains" and happy and companionable hours around the evening campfires. As Eveline Alexander's party neared Fort Union, she described the countryside as "the most beautiful on our route. ... We are encamped tonight in a bright, level valley, surrounded on all sides by mountains that raise their lofty heads protectingly over our camp. Now that we are in picturesque country I am no longer tired of marching." On the eastern end of the trail, Morris reported that their campground was on "a most beautiful Prairie, bordered on one side by low land, presenting altogether a very pleasing prospect." And, as the party neared the Arkansas River, she reported that "the Prairies are perfectly covered with flowers & beautiful ones too."[39]

Indeed, most of the women mentioned the beautiful wild flowers along parts of the route. Frances Boyd even admitted that despite their dangerous and painful barbs, the "cacti are really pretty ... in early spring, when they bloom. Then the bright-hued flowers dot the country with color, and relieve the eye." Indeed, Boyd came to love the country along the trail. "There is a rare and nameless charm in the contemplation of those extended prairies," she wrote, "with their soft gray tints, dreary to Eastern people, but so dearly loved by those who become imbued with the deep sentiment their vast expanse inspires."[40]

One of the most eloquent of the women, Julia Holmes, rhapsodized over the prairie country:

> With the blue sky overhead, the endless variety of flowers under foot, it seemed that the ocean's solitude had united with all the landscape beauties. In such a scene there is a peculiar charm for some minds, which it is impossible for me to describe; but it made my heart leap for joy.[41]

Holmes gloried in walking and riding across this beautiful country, and she quickly adopted the "reform dress" or bloomer costume introduced by feminist Amelia Bloomer in the 1850s. Holmes's trail clothing consisted of "a calico dress, reaching a little below the knee, pants of the same, Indian moccasins on my feet, and on my head a hat. However much it lacked in taste," she concluded, "I found it to be beyond value in comfort and convenience." Most of the women adopted simple and comfortable clothing for the journey, and one suspects that, like Eveline Alexander, they were less than thrilled at the prospect of having to return to hoop skirts and other impractical and uncomfortable fashions when they reached the end of their journey.[42]

It should be pointed out that travelers on the Santa Fe Trail, unlike those on the main emigrant roads, could break their journey at the various trading posts, ranches, and villages along the way. Although many of these were less than imposing, they did offer an opportunity to rest and procure fresh provisions. Alice Baldwin described Trinidad as a "squalid little town," but she also recorded the kindness and care shown her by two of the townswomen, Mrs. John D. Kinner and Señora Felipe Baca. Sister Mary Joanna was critical of most of the stage stations "beyond the line of civilization," but she reported that at one stop, despite the dust and disorder in their sleeping rooms, the dining room was a pleasant surprise. "There cleanliness and order prevailed," she noted. "It was a pleasure to see the hostess, all neatness, politeness [and] hospitality; and her savory dishes and snow-white table linen invited us to partake with delight the preparations."[43]

Overland travelers often complained of the plain and monotonous diet of bacon, beans, and bread which were the standard trail fare; in contrast, Santa Fe travelers were well supplied with fresh foods and vegetables. At Fort Harker, Baldwin stated, "[W]e secured ... fresh milk and loaves of bakers' bread—sweet and delicious—and a refreshing change from condensed milk and baking-powder biscuit." "We live ... first rate[,] have an abundance of milk & cream," Anna Morris wrote, and "the Dr ... brought me some nice little fish for my dinner." Ernestine Huning's party was particularly well fed, for she wrote of dining on "goose breast and truffles" and breakfasting on "potatoe salad, ham, and eggs, fresh butter and biscuit."[44]

In addition to reporting both the perils and pleasures of trail travel, the women also wrote extensively about the places they visited and the people they met. The women were perceptive observers, and they were curious and anxious to learn what they could of the area through which they traveled. They described the towns and villages in great detail, visited Indian camps and Mexican homes, and filled many of their pages with both praise and criticism about the Indian, Mexican, and Anglo residents of the trail.

I have written elsewhere about the women's ambivalent reactions to these trail residents, and time and space constraints prevent me from going into detail here. But in analyzing the women's reports on these various peoples one must bear in mind that the female journalists represented only a small group of travelers, and they often had a number of preconceived ideas and prejudices about the West and its residents which were reflected in their writing.[45] Nonetheless, when we attempt to record and interpret the experience of the Santa Fe Trail for our students, readers, and museum and library visitors, we must remember that not all the travelers on the trail were white, Anglo-Saxon males. There were many different travelers; they all had different experiences; and they all can add to our knowledge of the trail and its people. Women, like the menfolk, were travelers on the trail, and they deserve a place in its history.

Essays and Monographs

1
Merrill J. Mattes, *The Great Platte River Road: The Covered Wagon Mainline via Fort Kearny to Fort Laramie*, Nebraska State Historical Society Publications, vol. 25 (Lincoln: Nebraska State Historical Society, 1969), 523–65; Marc Simmons, "Women on the Santa Fe Trail: Diaries, Journals, Memoirs—An Annotated Bibliography," *New Mexico Historical Review* 61 (July 1986): 233–43.

2
Quoted in Joan M. Jensen and Darlis A. Miller, "The Gentle Tamers Revisited: New Approaches to the History of Women in the American West," *Pacific Historical Review* 49 (May 1980): 177.

3
T. A. Larson, "Women's Role in the American West," *Montana, the Magazine of Western History* 24 (Summer 1974): 4; Richard A. Bartlett, *The New Country: A Social History of the American Frontier, 1776–1890* (New York: Oxford University Press, 1974), 343.

4
Emerson Hough, *The Passing of the Frontier* (New Haven: Yale University Press, 1921), 93, and Everett Dick, "Sunbonnet and Calico, the Homesteader's Consort," *Nebraska History* 47 (March 1966): 13, both quoted in Glenda Riley, "Kansas Frontierswomen Viewed through Their Writings," *Kansas History* 9 (Spring 1986): 2; Marc Simmons, "Women on the Santa Fe Trail," typescript.

5
Cheryl J. Foote and Sandra K. Schackel, "Indian Women of New Mexico, 1535–1680," in Joan M. Jensen and Darlis A. Miller, eds., *New Mexico Women: Intercultural Perspectives* (Albuquerque: University of New Mexico Press, 1986), 22–23.

6
Ibid., 33.

7
Ibid., 32.

8
Janet Lecompte, *Pueblo, Hardscrabble, Greenhorn: The Upper Arkansas, 1832–1856* (Norman: University of Oklahoma Press, 1978), 63–65.

9
Ibid., 73.

10
Testimony of Calvin Jones, April 9, 1845, quoted in Lecompte, *Pueblo, Hardscrabble, Greenhorn*, 66.

11
Ibid., 66.

12
Ibid.

13
Marc Simmons, Afterword, *Land of Enchantment: Memoirs of Marian Russell along the Santa Fé Trail as Dictated to Mrs. Hal Russell* (Evanston, Ill.: Branding Iron Press, 1954; Albuquerque: University of New Mexico Press, 1984), 157–58.

14
Howard R. Lamar, Foreword to *Down the Santa Fe Trail and into Mexico: The Diary of Susan Shelby Magoffin, 1846–1847*, ed. Stella M. Drumm (New Haven: Yale University Press, 1926; Lincoln: University of Nebraska Press, Bison Books, 1982), xi–xvii.

15
Lydia Spencer Lane, *I Married a Soldier; or, Old Days in the Army* (Philadelphia: J. B. Lippincott Co., 1893; Albuquerque: Horn & Wallace, 1964); Introduction to Russell, *Land of Enchantment*, xii.

16
Eveline M. Alexander, *Cavalry Wife: The Diary of Eveline M. Alexander, 1866–1867*, ed. Sandra L. Myres (College Station: Texas A&M University Press, 1977).

17
Alice Blackwood Baldwin, *An Army Wife on the Frontier: The Memoirs of Alice Blackwood Baldwin, 1867–1877*, ed. Robert C. and Eleanor C. Carriker (Salt Lake City: Tanner Trust Fund, University of Utah Library, 1975); Mrs. Orsemus Bronson (Frances) Boyd, *Cavalry Life in Tent and Field* (New York: J. Selwin Tait & Sons, 1894; Lincoln: University of Nebraska Press, 1982).

18
Frances M. A. Mack Roe, *Army Letters from an Officer's Wife, 1871–1888* (New York: D. Appleton & Co., 1909; Lincoln: University of Nebraska Press, 1981); Elizabeth Bacon Custer, *Tenting on the Plains; or, General Custer in Kansas and Texas*, 3 vols. (New York: Harper & Brothers, 1895; Norman: University of Texas Press, 1971) and Minnie D. Millbrook, ed., "Mrs. General Custer at Fort Riley, 1866," *Kansas Historical Quarterly* 60 (Spring 1974): 63–71.

19
Josephine [McCrackin] Clifford, "An Officer's Wife in New Mexico," *Overland Monthly* 4 (February 1870): 152–60; Genevieve LaTourette, "Fort Union Memories," *New Mexico Historical Review* 26 (October 1951): 277–86; Anna Maria Morris, "A Military Wife on the Santa Fe Trail," in Kenneth L. Holmes, ed., *Covered Wagon Women: Diaries and Letters from the Western Trails, 1840–1890*, 5 vols. to date (Glendale, Calif.: Arthur H. Clark Company, 1983–1985), 2:15–43; Mrs. Byron N. Sanford, "Life at Camp Weld and Fort Lyon in 1861–62: An Extract from the Diary of Mrs. Byron N. Sanford," ed. Albert B. Sanford, *The Colorado Magazine* 7 (July 1930): 132–39; Ellen Williams, *Three Years and a Half in the Army; or, History of the Second Colorados* (New York: Fowler & Wells, 1885).

20
Harriet S. Kellogg, *Life of Mrs. Emily Harwood* (Albuquerque: El Abogado Press, 1903); Anna McKee, Letters, McKee Collection, box 414, Colorado Historical Society.

21
Sister M. Kotska Gauthreaux, ["Journey to Santa Fe, 1867"] in Thomas F. O'Connor, "Narratives of a Missionary Journey to New Mexico in 1867," *Mid-America* 19 (January 1937): 63–67; Mother Mary Magdalen Hayden, "Journey to Santa Fe, 1852," in Mary J. Straw, *Loretto: The Sisters and Their Chapel* (Santa Fe: Loretto Chapel Fund, 1983), 24–26; Rosa Maria (Sister Blandina) Segale, *At the End of the Santa Fe Trail* (Columbus, Ohio: Columbian Press, 1932; Milwaukee: Bruce Publishing Co., 1948); Sister Mary Joanna Welsh, "Sketch, Pioneering to Denver, Opening of the School, St. Mary's Academy, June 1864," Denver Public Library, Western History Collection.

22
Marc Simmons, "The Old Santa Fe Trail," *Overland Journal* 4 (Summer 1986): 68 (part 2 of a 3-part series).

23
Julia Archibald Holmes, *A Bloomer Girl on Pike's Peak, 1858*, ed. Agnes Wright Spring (Denver: Denver Public Library, 1949); Mamie (May Bell) Bernard Aguirre, "Spanish Trader's Bride," *Westport Historical Quarterly* 4 (December 1968): 5–23; Flora Spiegelberg, "Reminiscences of a Jewish Bride on the Santa Fe Trail," *Jewish Spectator* 2 (August 1937): 21–22, and ibid. 2 (September 1937): 24–25, 44; Ernestine Huning, "Trip across the Plains: Diary of Ernestine Huning," in Marc Simmons, ed., *On the Santa Fe Trail* (Lawrence: University of Kansas Press, 1986), all excerpts in this paper, however, are from a typescript of the diary kindly furnished me by Simmons; Susan E. Wallace,

The Land of the Pueblos (New York: George D. Hurst, 1888).

24
Morris, "Military Wife," 20, 27; Huning, "Trip across the Plains," typescript, 104.

25
Lane, *I Married a Soldier*, 43.

26
Alexander, *Cavalry Wife*, 37–38.

27
Baldwin, *Army Wife on the Frontier*, 28; Huning, "Trip across the Plains," 104–5.

28
Roe, *Army Letters*, 2; Welsh, "Sketch."

29
Wallace, *Land of the Pueblos*, 8, 12.

30
Welsh, "Sketch"; Magoffin, *Down the Santa Fe Trail*, 34.

31
Baldwin, *Army Wife on the Frontier*, 47.

32
Lane, *I Married a Soldier*, 49–50.

33
Ibid., 51.

34
Baldwin, *Army Wife on the Frontier*, 54.

35
Boyd, *Cavalry Life*, 173; Morris, "Military Wife," 134.

36
Boyd, *Cavalry Life*, 173; Lane, *I Married a Soldier*, 47.

37
Huning, "Trip across the Plains," typescript, 107; Magoffin, *Down the Santa Fe Trail*, 69; Baldwin, *Army Wife on the Frontier*, 59.

38
Baldwin, *Army Wife on the Frontier*, 25, 55; Welsh, "Sketch."

39
Alexander, *Cavalry Wife*, 73–74; Morris, "Military Wife," 21, 28.

40
Boyd, *Cavalry Life*, 175.

41
Holmes, *Bloomer Girl*, 15.

42
Ibid., 16; Alexander, *Cavalry Wife*, 71–72.

43
Baldwin, *Army Wife on the Frontier*, 54; Welsh, "Sketch."

44
Baldwin, *Army Wife on the Frontier*, 54; Morris, "Military Wife," 23; Huning, "Trip across the Plains," typescript, 103, 106.

45
See Sandra L. Myres, "The Ladies of the Army—Views of Western Life," in *The American Military on the Frontier: Proceedings of the Seventh Military History Symposium, USAF Academy, 1976* (Washington, D.C.: Office of Air Force History and United States Air Force Academy, 1978), 135–53, and "Romance and Reality on the American Frontier: Views of Army Wives," *Western Historical Quarterly* 13 (October 1982): 409–27.

ESSAY FOUR

Barton H. Barbour

James Ross Larkin
A Well-Heeled Health Seeker
on the Santa Fe Trail, 1856–57

About the author
Barton H. Barbour is presently completing a Ph.D. dissertation in the Department of History at the University of New Mexico. He has worked for several museums in New Mexico and for the National Park Service at Bent's Old Fort National Historic Site. His books include *Tales of the Mountain Men* (1984), *Edward Warren* (1986), and *Reluctant Frontiersman: James Ross Larkin on the Santa Fe Trail, 1856–57* (University of New Mexico Press, 1990), which received a 1991 Award of Merit from the Santa Fe Trail Association.

Essays and Monographs

In 1984, while he was employed as a museum curator at Bent's Old Fort National Historic Site, Barton H. Barbour cataloged a historical collection consisting mostly of objects on display at the reconstructed fort. While in this process, he discovered an original diary kept by James Ross Larkin that had found its way into the collection. The leather-bound journal, measuring four inches by six inches and about a half inch thick, contained the diary of a heretofore unknown Santa Fe Trail traveler. It was loaned to the National Park Service in 1979 by Larkin's great-grandson, a retired lawyer then living in Pensacola, Florida. Eventually, in 1980 the diary, along with a carte de visite *and some minor additional materials, was donated without restriction to the National Park Service. The Larkin materials were sent to the Denver regional office and then to Bent's Old Fort, where they were placed in a safe and left for several years.*

THE SANTA FE TRAIL has provided inspiration for dozens of scholarly and popular works of history for well over a century. The firsthand accounts of William Becknell, Thomas James, George C. Sibley, Josiah Gregg, and James Josiah Webb have given trail scholars a view of the early years of trail life and adventure. However, the decade of the 1850s has been generally overlooked by historians. The diary of James Ross Larkin belongs to that neglected decade in Santa Fe Trail studies.

James Ross Larkin was born in Wilmington, Delaware, on July 23, 1831, the son of Thomas Henry Larkin and Susan Ross Glasgow. Later, in St. Louis, his father made a living as a purveyor of goods and supplies for the fur trade and the Santa Fe traders.[1] James's mother was a member of an important St. Louis mercantile family, and the combined family connections enabled James to make the trip to New Mexico armed with numerous letters of introduction to people of substance in the territory. His cousins the Glasgow brothers, for example, penned a letter of introduction to the firm of Webb and Kingsbury of Santa Fe indicating that James would be visiting that city for health reasons. Among other notables to whom Larkin secured letters of introduction were Henry Connelly, Hugh Stephenson, Ceran St. Vrain, Judge Joab Houghton, James L. Collins, and Carlos (Charles) Beaubien.

Recent discovery of additional manuscript materials in the Missouri Historical Society will shed light on Larkin's life following his western odyssey. It is known that he married Mary Chambers

James Ross Larkin

(1833–1918) on October 19, 1859. Widowed seven years previous to her marriage to James at the age of twenty-four, Mary Chambers Larkin was remembered as a model Catholic who was able to bring her new husband into the fold. Of the eight children from this marriage, six survived. One of the daughters, Annie, was the grandmother of Philip Beall, Jr., who donated the diary to the National Park Service in 1979. Mary Larkin outlived her second husband by more than forty years, for James died in 1874.

James Ross Larkin was but one of many people who took to the Santa Fe Trail to bolster flagging health. By 1856 the salubrious climate of New Mexico was well enough publicized to convince the invalid diarist to forego a trip to the mountains of Virginia and take the trail to Santa Fe. Larkin's family connections aided in the orchestration of his voyage, and he was fortunate to have William Bent as his guide. On September 18, 1856, Larkin notes "having returned home Sep 14th from a trip to Cape May[,] Catskill Mts, Nahant, & Rockbridge[,] Alum Springs &c in search of better health & not being permanently cured, I find my mother and some of my friends desire me to go out in the Plains of New Mexico. I accordingly visited Mr Wm Bent, a noted Indian Trader, & he consented that I should go out in his train to his Fort—Known as Bent's Fort—situated on the Arkansas river."[2]

Unlike many health seekers, Larkin suffered not from tubercular problems; rather, he seems to have been dyspeptic, both in the literal and in the figurative sense. Among the symptoms that variously beset him were costiveness, or constipation, diarrhea, indigestion, and rheumatism. On October 4, 1856, after a buffalo hunt with William Bent, he writes: "I felt better from the excitement. (I have been very costive for several days, & today had a tremendous passage & am much improved [)] It seems persons frequently become costive in starting across, but I felt no great inconvenience from it as I would have felt at home."[3] Larkin states that eating some Mexican molasses had made him "quite unwell," and other foods had a deleterious effect on his weak digestive system. His prescription for his stomach discomfort was some "fine brandy" obtained from Jose Play, at Mora.[4]

James Ross Larkin traveled the Santa Fe Trail in 1856–57 and wrote daily journal entries during his journey, recording his experiences on the trail while traveling in the caravan of the famed fur trader and entrepreneur William Bent. His observations of Bent and his Cheyenne wife, Yellow Woman,[5] shed some additional light on the aging frontiersman's personality as well as on the trade at Bent's New Fort. In addition, Larkin encountered people and described places that are not well known in the literature of the trail. A uniquely valuable aspect of his diary is an excellent inventory list and cost accounting for each article taken on the tour. Larkin's inventory gives a singularly fine view of the camp equipment, clothing, and gear used on the trail, though he was doubtless more lavishly supplied than many trail wanderers. His total outlay of funds for the five-month venture amounted to nearly $1,200, a considerable sum in that day.

Larkin left St. Louis on September 19, 1856, after making hasty preparations for his departure with William Bent's caravan for that year. He rolled out of St. Louis on the Pacific Railroad[6] to Jefferson City, on the banks of the Missouri, where he was to board the steamer *Morning Star*, known in the trade as "Tom Brierly's floating palace." Three days and several groundings later the *Morning Star* landed at Westport, or "Kansas." It was here that Larkin joined Bent's caravan on September 25. The party consisted of "Americans, Mexicans, French, Germans & Pawnee Indians—numbering about 16 men. We also have Mr Bents Lady, an Indian woman—the 'old Scwaw' [sic] as he calls her, & also her pet—a little Pawnee Indian who was a prisoner... bot [sic] by Mr Bent."[7]

During the westward trek along the Santa Fe Trail, the outfit camped at most of the standard spots used by the traders, duly noted by the diarist. He also observed some of the border conflict that presaged the coming Civil War in "Bleeding Kansas." As he passed Lawrence, the Kansas headquarters of the abolitionist Emigrant Aid Company, Larkin notes on September 27:

> Today we passed in sight of Lawrence & are now within about 12 miles of it. Within past 2 days we have passed houses uninhabited on account of the Kansas difficulties, & some that have been burned. One was burning as we passed. Almost every one living on the road has been plundered, robbed or driven away by one side or the other—Missourians or Freesoilers. The country is in an awful condition at present, no one knowing how long his house, goods or stock may be safe from the maurauders [sic].[8]

From October 13 to 27 Larkin stayed at Bent's New Fort, near present Lamar, Colorado, some thirty-five miles from the more famous Bent's Old Fort. Larkin describes in his diary the appearance of the fort, a rarity in Santa Fe Trail literature. "Bent's Fort," he states, "is situated on the north side of the Arkansas River on a bold bluff.... It is built of brown sandstone—being about 170 feet long and 80 feet wide. The walls are about 14 feet high, & the houses are ranged around the inside—leaving a large open space in center."[9]

During his sojourn at the new fort, Larkin witnessed a serious altercation between William Bent and one of Bent's employees, a "Frenchman" of as yet unknown identity, that nearly ended in bloodshed. It seems that the employee had given whiskey to some Kiowas during Bent's absence in order to enhance his standing among them. Bent dismissed the Frenchman, after which Larkin writes: "Many angry words passed, in by no means a peaceable manner, & Mr Bent struck the Frenchman one or two blows & drove him out of the Fort, giving him a kick before his Kioway friend, & accompanying it with an insulting remark."[10]

Though Bent planned to sell his fort to the government, Larkin fails to record anything concerning the proposed sale. Only a few weeks before Larkin joined his wagon train, while at Westport on August 25, 1856, Bent had written a letter to Major George C. Waffman, Commandant of Subsistence, at St. Louis in which he offered the fort for sale and requested that the many tons of government provisions stored there be "removed or disposed of in some way."[11] Had word about the whiskey incident reached government officials, Bent's chance to sell the fort might have been jeopardized.

Larkin was also on hand to hear of troubles with the Cheyennes that eventually precipitated a punitive campaign in 1857 against that tribe under the leadership of Colonel E. V. Sumner. On October 5 Larkin writes, "Mr. B.[ent] informed them of the report that reached Sts. [States] before we started, that a number of their tribe had been killed & taken prisoner at or near Fort Laramie by the U.S. Troops, but they had not or pretended not to have heard of it, & looked quite serious on learning it."[12]

By October 27 Larkin was again en route to Santa Fe. He passed Bent's Old Fort on the twenty-eighth and left a description of the moldering but not totally abandoned post. He remarks in his diary that it was "now in ruins, having been set on fire several times. It was once quite an imposing fort built of adobe, but is now much dilapidated. A number of Mexicans were camping there."[13]

After following Timpas Creek past the Three Buttes and on to the "Picketware" (Purgatoire) River, Larkin's party on November 1 began the ascent of Raton Pass, the most difficult part of the trip for wagons. Once over the pass, Larkin visited a "very polite & hospitable" Lucien Maxwell at his hacienda on Rayado Creek, where the diarist met but regrettably failed to describe or comment on the soon-to-be famous Kit Carson, whose first biography would appear in two years.[14]

Larkin continued on to Mora and enjoyed the hospitality at the home of Jose Play. Here he attended his first fandango, which he described as "a novel affair.... [E]very one almost was there. The Mexicans dance very gracefully—They are smoking almost all the time. Had a barroom attached to the large dansing [sic] room, where much liquor was drank, & a Monte Bank attended by a woman was in full operation. A gent asks any lady to dance."[15]

In Las Vegas Larkin stayed at the house of the local padre, who, he writes, "entertained us very hospitably, brot out his wines & seemed to be quite a bon vivant. He was formerly a French soldier, & changed from that to a Priest—but is certainly more fit for the former. I drank some Mexican wine with him—& was quite sick afterwards—with pain & frequent discharges. After taking some paregoric I was relieved."[16]

Larkin passed the Pecos ruin, recorded his version of the tale concerning Montezuma and the perpetual fire that has been noted by several writers,[17] and eventually reached Santa Fe. Upon arriving there on November 15, he checked into La Fonda, or the Exchange Hotel. He writes: "The house is very well kept—their table being really excellent, supplied with almost every thing the country affords—immense onions, beets, cabbages, rather small potatoes &c. The fare is high being $2.50 per day for board and lodging & $1.00 per horse—rather costly."[18] But such was required by the young Missourian, for after all, the Fonda was "the place of rendezvous for the better class of Americans."

Larkin was soon at home among the ranking military society of Santa Fe, and on December 30 he was offered a job as a paymaster's clerk by Major Albert Smith. As his first act on the job, Larkin started on December 31 with a party of six soldiers and Major Smith to Fort Union, where he arrived on January 2 and met many of the officers present. After paying off the troops, his party left Fort Union on January 5 for Santa Fe. His arrival at Santa Fe coincided with a celebration of the Eighth of January, commemorating the Battle of New Orleans.

The diarist remained at Santa Fe socializing with the officers and their wives until at least January 31, 1857, when the diary abruptly ends. By this time Larkin had sold his mules and ambulance to Thomas Bowler, "of Green & Bowler" and made arrangements to settle his debt to William Bent. Presumably he was ready to return to St. Louis, but thus far no journal for the trip has been discovered.

A recent research venture by the author to St. Louis resulted in the identification of four additional manuscript diaries kept by Larkin that illuminate his later life but do not add to his trail experiences. As research continues, he hopes to produce a biography of James Ross Larkin and to annotate his journal with the aim of placing it within the context of other noteworthy Santa Fe Trail journals.

[1] Sublette Papers, Missouri Historical Society, index card referencing T. H. Larkin for the year 1843.

[2] James Ross Larkin, manuscript diary, Bent's Old Fort National Historic Site, 12 (hereafter Larkin MS).

[3] Ibid., 28.

[4] Ibid., 68.

[5] This would be Bent's second Cheyenne wife, the sister of Owl Woman, who died in childbirth in July 1847. See David Lavender, *Bent's Fort* (Garden City, N.Y.: Doubleday & Co., 1954), 301–2.

[6] The Pacific Railroad of Missouri, or the Missouri Pacific, was chartered by the Missouri state legislature in March 1849, just one month after U.S. Senator Thomas Hart Benton had introduced a bill to locate and build a national highway from the Mississippi River to the Pacific. Missouri began the great work at St. Louis in 1851 and by 1855 the railroad had reached Jefferson City; the line reached Kansas City ten years later. See John D. Cruise, "Early Days on the Union Pacific," in *Kansas Historical Collections* 9 (Topeka: State Printing Office, 1910): 529–49.

[7] Larkin MS, 22.

[8] Ibid., 20

[9] Ibid., 38–39.

[10] Ibid., 43.

[11] Nolie Mumey, *Old Forts and Trading Posts of the West: Bent's Old Fort and Bent's New Fort of the Arkansas River* (Denver: Artcraft Press, 1956), 133 ff.

[12] Larkin MS, 31–32.

[13] Ibid., 56–57.

[14] See DeWitt C. Peters, M.D., *The Life and Adventures of Kit Carson, the Nestor of the Rocky Mountains* (New York: Clark & Meeker, 1859).

[15] Larkin MS, 74.

[16] Ibid., 98.

[17] See John L. Kessell, *Kiva, Cross, and Crown: The Pecos Indians and New Mexico, 1540-1840* (Washington: Government Printing Office, 1979), 459-63.

[18] Larkin MS, 73.

ESSAY FIVE

Janet Lecompte

The Mountain Branch
Raton Pass and Sangre de Cristo Pass

About the author
A scholar of early western history, Janet Lecompte contributed nearly three dozen articles to *The Mountain Men and the Fur Trade of the Far West* and has written many journal articles on aspects of Colorado and the Southwest. She has published three books: *Pueblo, Hardscrabble, Greenhorn: The Upper Arkansas, 1832–1856* (1978), *Rebellion in Rio Arriba, 1837* (1985), and *Emily: The Diary of a Hard-Worked Woman* (1987). At present she is writing a study of New Mexico in the Mexican period.

THE TRAIL from the settlements of Missouri to Santa Fe branched in western Kansas. The principal route made a beeline for Santa Fe, cutting diagonally across the Cimarron desert; the other route continued west up the Arkansas to Bent's Fort, then up Timpas Creek to the foot of the Raton Mountains at Trinidad, Colorado, across the mountains over Raton Pass, and down to present Raton, New Mexico. In eastern New Mexico it merged with the principal route now known as the Santa Fe Trail. The Bent's Fort branch is now called the Mountain Branch. But neither "Santa Fe Trail " nor "Mountain Branch" were terms in common use until the 1860s, although almost every historian of the Santa Fe Trail assumes that they were.[1]

A motorist on the present four-lane highway over Raton Pass (altitude 7,888), a distance of twenty-five miles, can drive it in about half an hour. It is now one of the easiest passes through the mountains, but it was not always so. Nor was it, as guide books and road signs state, the only or even the principal route between Colorado and New Mexico in the early days. This paper is an attempt to determine when and in what form the Mountain Branch began; how much of its travel went over Raton Pass; and what part the Sangre de Cristo Pass played in trail history.

The Mountain Branch over Raton Pass was safer than the more popular Cimarron route, less exposed to Indian attack and to death in the Cimarron desert for lack of wood, water, and grass. But it was a hundred miles longer, and its Raton Pass segment was a major obstacle. Raton Pass was arduous for men on foot; for men with wagons, horses, and mules it was a torment. Before a road was built over the pass in 1866, scarcely a wagon train on this route could avoid lamed animals, overturned wagons with broken axles, ruptured baggage and goods scattered in the creek bed—not to mention serious loss of time. Consequently, Raton Pass was little used until the Mexican War of 1846–48.

The Raton Mountains are a series of high mesas adjoining the Sangre de Cristo Mountains at right angles and running east along the Colorado–New Mexico state line for a hundred miles before sinking into the plains. The mesas are divided by narrow and precipitous canyons clogged with roots and branches and blocked by huge boulders. Through some of these canyons the Indians had narrow trails. Raton Pass, as well as an unnamed route west of it, and four gaps east of it (San Francisco Pass, Manco de Burro Pass,

Trinchera Pass, and Emery Gap) had trails that were all considered difficult if not impassable for wagons.[2]

Other mountain passes leading to New Mexico crossed the Sangre de Cristo Mountains, which run north and south from the Arkansas River to the plains east of Santa Fe. The earliest Spaniards, knowing no better, crossed two difficult passes in going to the Arkansas Valley where friendly Apaches lived. Ulibarri in 1706, Valverde in 1719, and probably Villasur in 1720 took their little companies of soldiers and militia from Santa Fe to Taos, then over the Taos or Palo Flechado Pass through the Sangre de Cristo Mountains onto the plains of northeastern New Mexico, and then through the Raton Mountains into southeastern Colorado. The only eighteenth-century Spanish officer certain to have used Raton Pass was New Mexico's Governor Antonio Valverde y Cosio with his expedition of 1719. His report described Raton Pass as "so many forests, ravines, canyons, and narrow places that it was necessary that day to divide the cavalry into ten groups to get over such a difficult trail."[3] From that time on, Spaniards used a better route.

The better route, discovered by Comanches, was through the Sangre de Cristo Mountains. In the 1720s Comanches swept down from the north, driving the friendly Apaches from the Arkansas Valley, raiding New Mexican towns and ranches, and trading with the Taos Indians. Their route to New Mexico crossed the Sangre de Cristo Mountains diagonally by ascending a branch of the Huerfano River to the top of the Sangre de Cristo Pass, down Sangre de Cristo Creek to the San Luis Valley, and south to Taos. The trail was gradual in grade, smooth, and wide in most places; men on horseback could travel from the site of present Pueblo via the Sangre de Cristo Pass to Taos in three days.[4]

From the 1730s until 1763 (when France relinquished claim to Louisiana Territory), French traders from the Mississippi Valley supplied the Comanches with arms. Some French traders lived in Comanche villages in the Arkansas Valley and came to Taos and Santa Fe occasionally, only to be arrested and their goods confiscated by Spanish soldiers, for Spain allowed no foreign commerce in colonial New Mexico. The routes of these traders are in doubt, except for four Louisiana Frenchmen who testified in Santa Fe that they had left their trading post among the Comanches on the Arkansas in the fall of 1749, crossed to the San Luis Valley by the Sangre de Cristo Pass, and were guided to Taos by Comanches.[5]

In the last half of the eighteenth century, Spaniards seemed to use the Sangre de Cristo route into the Arkansas Valley to the exclusion of any other route. In July 1768 New Mexican Governor Pedro Fermin de Mendinueta led an expedition of 546 men through Taos and the Sangre de Cristo Pass to the Arkansas Valley to punish the Comanches. His successor, Governor Juan Bautista de Anza, and hundreds of soldiers returned to New Mexico via the Sangre de Cristo Pass in the summer of 1779 after defeating Chief Greenhorn's Comanches in the Arkansas Valley. For months after Anza's victory, Spanish workmen and materials were brought over the Sangre de Cristo trail to build a town for the Comanches on or near the Arkansas, which the Indians abandoned a few months after its completion. In 1786 Governor Anza made peace with the numerous Comanches. After this treaty New Mexican soldiers, hunters, and traders safely entered the Arkansas Valley via the Sangre de Cristo Pass.[6]

For many years the traffic of Spaniards and Indians over the Sangre de Cristo Pass deepened its trail ruts. In 1804 the United States bought Louisiana, a territory of unknown dimension except that one of its southern boundaries was the Arkansas River. Henceforth New Mexico was visited by American trappers and traders. The first were James Pursley in 1804 and Baptiste Lalande in 1805, who were probably escorted by Indians over the Sangre de Cristo Pass, but records of their routes are vague.[7]

In 1807 Lieutenant Zebulon M. Pike's party came up the Arkansas River to explore the southern boundaries of the Louisiana Purchase and crossed Medano (Sand Hill) Pass over the Sangre de Cristo Mountains into the San Luis Valley. There they were arrested by Spaniards and escorted to Santa Fe (where Pike found Pursley and Lalande comfortably settled). Pike's party was sent to Chihuahua and finally allowed to go home. Alarmed by Pike's intrusion, Governor Alencaster in 1807 ordered lookouts placed on the Sangre de Cristo Pass and on Fountain River (Rio Almagre or Fontaine-qui-bouille) described as four days' journey from Taos.[8]

Pike's report mentioned the New Mexicans' need for goods, which encouraged American traders to come to New Mexico. Those who did were arrested and their goods confiscated. In 1810 James McLanahan, Reuben Smith, and James Patterson were arrested and imprisoned for several years in the Presidio of San Eleazario. The same fate befell two other parties in 1812, one led by James Baird,

Robert McKnight, and Samuel Chambers and the other a party of Manuel Lisa's traders from the Upper Missouri River. These would-be merchants left no records, but all appeared first in Taos, indicating that they, too, probably came over Sangre de Cristo Pass.[9]

Later traders and trappers on the Upper Arkansas left records describing their routes. Joseph Philibert and his eighteen St. Louis French trappers worked on the Arkansas and in the San Luis Valley in 1814–15 and wintered in Taos. Philibert described Taos as "on the road to their former hunting camp" indicating that they had come over the Sangre de Cristo Pass. Between 1815 and 1817 Auguste Chouteau and Jules DeMun with their trappers made frequent trips from the Arkansas Valley to Taos over the same pass. They were finally arrested, deprived of their goods and furs, and sent home to St. Louis.[10]

Spanish officials in New Mexico were deeply concerned about these Americans, suspecting that they were supplying hostile Plains Indians in the Arkansas Valley with guns and ammunition. In 1818 Lieutenant Jose Maria de Arce was sent with militia from Taos over the Sangre de Cristo Pass (his journal calls it "The Gap of the Sierra Blanca") to reconnoiter the Arkansas Valley. Finding no Americans, Arce returned over the Raton Mountains via San Francisco Pass and down Chicorica Creek to the Canadian River (Rio Colorado).[11]

In 1819 Governor Melgares was alarmed to receive an anonymous report (actually written by Jules DeMun in 1818) describing the Sangre de Cristo Pass as practicable for artillery with a little work, a place where a handful of men could hold off an entire army. The governor was also alarmed by General O'Fallen's expedition of 1818 to the mouth of the Yellowstone River and by James Long's reported invasion of Texas. He ordered a reconnaissance of the Yellowstone and fortifications built in the Sangre de Cristo Pass and the Canon de San Fernando near Taos. In 1819 he ordered a fort built on the eastern side of the Sangre de Cristo Pass, which was attacked and destroyed six months later by Indians (or by Americans dressed as Indians, as the sole Spanish survivor reported). The governor sent 300 men to reinforce the fort and punish the Indians, but the fort was soon abandoned.[12]

In 1821 Mexico declared her independence of Spain and opened her borders to foreign commerce. One of her first American traders was William Becknell of Franklin, Missouri, who brought his pack train along the Arkansas, up the steep and difficult valley of the Purgatoire and over the Raton Mountains, complaining all the way. Historians have assumed that Becknell's passage of the mountains was over Raton Pass, but another look at the route suggests that Becknell went over Trinchera Pass, to the east of Raton Pass. Becknell's journal was published on his return, describing his route as presenting "difficulties almost insurmountable." This judgment against the route may have kept Missouri traders away from the Mountain Branch for a score of years to come. Becknell himself avoided the Raton Mountains on his return journey to Missouri by cutting across the plains to the Cimarron River, which became the principal route of the Santa Fe Trail from 1821 until the railroad usurped its function in 1880.[13]

Trade between frontier merchants of Missouri and customers at Santa Fe developed rapidly in the 1820s; pack trains became wagon trains, and small parties of traders became great caravans of several hundred wagons. Until the middle 1830s all commercial travel was along the Cimarron route.[14] As American wagons reached Santa Fe from the plains, American trappers crept into Taos from the mountains with their beaver and marketed it secretly at that remote northerly town, for few of them had the governor's permission to trap. Probably these trappers kept to the mountains and used the Sangre de Cristo Pass to and from the Arkansas River, but they left few records of their travels or clandestine operations.[15]

In 1832 John Gantt opened trade with the Cheyenne and Arapaho Indians on the Arkansas, at the mouth of the Purgatoire. He bought at least some of his supplies in Taos, and he used the Sangre de Cristo Pass to get there. In 1833 both Gantt and Charles Bent built trading posts near the present site of Pueblo. Vigorous competition from the Bents soon drove Gantt away. By the spring of 1835 Bent's Fort was in operation near present La Junta, Colorado, and for the next fourteen years it dominated the Indian trade of the region.[16]

The Indian trade at Bent's Fort on the Arkansas, however, was only part of the Bents' business. They also brought trade goods from Missouri along the Cimarron Branch of the Santa Fe Trail to sell in Santa Fe, or took them south to sell in the interior of Mexico. At various times they had stores in Taos as well as in Santa Fe and in a village north of Taos called Rio Colorado (near present Questa). The Santa Fe store was supplied by wagon trains on the Cimarron route, but supplies for the stores at Taos and Rio Colorado were probably brought from Bent's Fort over the Sangre de Cristo Pass.[17]

In the 1830s almost all travel between the Arkansas Valley and New Mexico appears to have been over the Sangre de Cristo Pass, but a single account confirms that as early as 1839 Raton Pass saw some travel from Bent's Fort. Matt Field, editor of the *New Orleans Picayune*, wrote a sketch for his newspaper entitled "The Ratone." Field described his one-day passage over Raton Pass in the summer of 1839 as complicated by cliffs and precipices, heavy rocks, overhanging branches and projecting roots, making this day "perhaps the most wretchedly uncomfortable of our whole journey."[18]

The Arkansas Valley settlements of Pueblo, Hardscrabble, and Greenhorn were established in the 1840s and the comings and goings between these settlements and Taos over the Sangre de Cristo Pass were frequent. The people of the Arkansas Valley settlements bought flour and whiskey for sale to the Indians on the Arkansas and made regular visits to family and friends, since most of them were natives of Taos.[19]

In 1845 Lieutenant James B. Abert and a party of soldiers left Bent's Fort for Raton Pass and New Mexico in an apparent rehearsal for the American invasion of New Mexico the next year. Abert describes the trail over Raton Pass as "but recently commenced" and "an exceedingly rough route," so narrow that his party had to travel at times in the creek bed itself.[20]

Rough as the Raton Pass road was, it was relatively safe; Colonel Stephen H. Kearny and the War Department chose this route for invading New Mexico in August 1846, at the beginning of the Mexican War. Major Emory ordered the first troops to "clear the road," but if they did so, it made little difference to those who followed. John T. Hughes, a soldier in Colonel Doniphan's regiment, wrote of Raton Pass in 1846: "This day's march was extremely arduous and severe on our teams. Rough roads and rocky hills obstructed our progress." Colonel Doniphan granted his exhausted men a day's rest after they had crossed the pass.[21]

Close behind Kearny's army came a train of traders' wagons with Susan Magoffin, the young wife of one of the traders. Magoffin's diary chronicles the five days it took to cross Raton Pass and the miseries thereof. On the third day she wrote, "Still in the Raton, traveling on at the rate of half a mile an hour, with the road growing worse and worse."[22]

Thirteen years later the road was still wretched. Luis Baca, who led Hispanic colonists to the Purgatoire Valley in 1860, wrote of Raton Pass: "Here they had no roads; they were trails. Some of the slopes on the sides were at an angle of about 45 degrees... several wagons rolled over." Also in 1860, Marian Russell found the Raton Pass road "steep and tortuous ... little better than a faint wheel mark among the Pines... six wagons with broken axles."[23]

In 1865 Richens ("Uncle Dick") Wootton obtained charters from the Colorado and New Mexico legislatures to build a toll road over Raton Pass from Trinidad to the Red (Canadian) River. Wootton wrote of Raton Pass:

> A trail led through the canon it is true, but that was almost impassable for anything but saddle horses and pack animals at any time, and entirely impassable for wagon trains or stages in the winter time. ... There were hillsides to cut down, rocks to blast and remove, and bridges to build by the score. I built the road, however, and made it a good one too.[24]

After Wootton completed his toll road in 1866, it was used by stage companies, freighters, troops and supplies, and tourists at all seasons of the year. Wootton's road became the principal artery between Colorado and New Mexico until 1880, when the railroad was built over Raton Pass.[25]

In the meantime, the Sangre de Cristo Pass road fell into disuse. The Denver and Rio Grande Railroad bypassed it and blasted a route through nearby La Veta Pass in 1877–78 in order to serve its coal towns of La Veta and Walsenburg. The old La Veta Pass road ascended the Cucharas River south of the Huerfano River, and, like the Sangre de Cristo trail, descended Sangre de Cristo Creek into the San Luis Valley.[26]

At present, a new La Veta Pass road has a four-lane highway over it, but Sangre de Cristo Pass road has only faint marks on various parcels of fenced private land. Near the top of La Veta Pass on either side of the highway the ruts of the old Sangre de Cristo trail run up the hill and down the valley. These ruts should be marked and preserved, for they signify a century or more of travel before the Santa Fe Trail, the Mountain Branch, or Raton Pass became prominent in the West.

The Mountain Branch

1
Neither "Santa Fe Trail" nor "Mountain Branch" was used by prominent journalists of the Santa Fe Trail— Josiah Gregg in *Commerce of the Prairies,* James Josiah Webb in *Adventures in the Santa Fe Trade,* Matt Field in *Matt Field on the Santa Fe Trail,* Susan Magoffin in *Down the Santa Fe Trail and into Mexico,* and the military reports of Lieutenant James W. Abert in 1845 and 1846 and of Major W. H. Emory in 1846. Nor did I find documentary reference (although plenty of editorial reference) to those names in a cursory survey of Reuben Gold Thwaites's series *Early Western Travels* and LeRoy Hafen's *Southwest Historical Series* and *Far West and Rockies Historical Series.* The earliest reference to "Santa Fe Trail" I have found is in an emigrant guidebook of 1859, and the "Mountain Branch" did not show up in print until the 1860s—but a more dedicated researcher may well prove me in error. Travelers on the two branches of the trail before the 1850s generally called them the "road to Santa Fe" and the "Bent's Fort road."

2
Howard Louis Conard, *"Uncle Dick" Wootton: The Pioneer Frontiersman of the Rocky Mountain Region* (Chicago: W. E. Dibble & Co., 1890; Time-Life Books: 1980), 418; William A. Bell, *New Tracks in North America: A Journal of Travel and Adventure Whilst Engaged in the Survey for a Southern Railroad to the Pacific Ocean during 1867-8* (London: Chapman & Hall, 1869), 1:94-95.

3
A. B. Thomas, trans. and ed., *After Coronado: Spanish Exploration Northeast of New Mexico, 1696-1727; Documents from the Archives of Spain, Mexico, and New Mexico* (Norman: University of Oklahoma Press, 1935), 116. Alfred Barnaby Thomas's *After Coronado* is the standard source for translations of journals of seventeenth-century Spanish travelers, but his interpretation of their routes is often questionable. For other interpretations, see James H. Gunnerson, "Documentary Clues and Northeastern New Mexico Archeology," *Papers of the Philmont Conference on the Archeology of Northeastern New Mexico,* ed. Carol J. Condie; *New Mexico Archeological Council Proceedings* 6, (1984): 49-66; and Albert H. Schroeder, "A Study of the Apache Indians," part II, "The Jicarilla Apaches," typescript (Santa Fe, 1958), 20-44.

4
Elizabeth A. H. John, *Storms Brewed in Other Men's Worlds: The Confrontation of Indians, Spanish, and French in the Southwest, 1540-1795* (College Station, Tex.: Texas A&M University Press, 1975), 230-58; Ruth Marie Colville, "The Sangre de Cristo Trail," *The San Luis Valley Historian* 4 (Winter 1972): 11-13. Other trails through the Sangre de Cristo Mountains into the San Luis Valley were over Mosca (Robidoux) Pass, Medano (Sand Hill) Pass, and Music Pass.

5
Extracto, Provincias Internas, vol. 37, exp. 2, ff 21-14, Bolton Collection, Bancroft Library, University of California, Berkeley. For other French trading parties see John, *Storms Brewed in Other Men's Worlds,* 313-21; Ralph Emerson Twitchell, *The Spanish Archives of New Mexico* (Cedar Rapids, Iowa: The Torch Press, 1914), 1:148-51 and 2:214; Herbert E. Bolton, "French Intrusions into New Mexico, 1749-1752," *Bolton and the Spanish Borderlands* (Norman: University of Oklahoma Press, 1964), 155-64.

6
Alfred Barnaby Thomas, ed., *The Plains Indians and New Mexico,*

1751-1778: A Collection of Documents Illustrative of the History of the Eastern Frontier of New Mexico (Albuquerque: University of New Mexico Press, 1940), 150–62, 167; Alfred Barnaby Thomas, *Forgotten Frontiers: A Study of the Spanish Indian Policy of Don Juan Bautista de Anza, Governor of New Mexico, 1777–1787, from the Original Documents in the Archives of Spain, Mexico, and New Mexico* (Norman: University of Oklahoma Press, 1932), map opp. p. 1., 134–37; Alfred B. Thomas, "San Carlos: A Comanche Pueblo on the Arkansas River, 1787," *The Colorado Magazine* 6 (May 1929): 79–91.

7
Janet Lecompte, "James Pursley," in LeRoy R. Hafen ed., *The Mountain Men and the Fur Trade of the Far West: Biographical Sketches of the Participants by Scholars of the Subject and with Introductions by the Editor* (Glendale, Calif.: The Arthur H. Clark Company, 1971), 8:282–83; Richard E. Oglesby, "Baptiste LaLande," *Mountain Men and the Fur Trade*, 6:218–22; Gov. Wilkinson to the secretary of war, St. Louis, August 10, 1805, in Clarence E. Carter, *The Territorial Papers of the United States* (Washington, DC.: U.S. Government Printing Office, 1948), 13:182–83; Fray Angelico Chavez, "Addenda to New Mexico Families," *El Palacio* 63 (July-August, 1956): 242.

8
Donald Jackson, ed., *The Journals of Zebulon Montgomery Pike with Letters and Related Documents* (Norman: University of Oklahoma Press, 1966) 1:290–448; Gov. Real Alencaster, Santa Fe, April 18, 1807, *Spanish Archives of New Mexico* (hereafter *SANM*) microfilm publication, New Mexico State Archives, roll 16, frames 324–32.

9
Gov. Manrrique to Gov. Salcedo, Santa Fe, March 31, 1810, *SANM*, roll 17, frames 75–84; Rex W. Strickland, "James Baird," in *Mountain Men and the Fur Trade*, 3:28; Herbert E. Bolton, "New Light on Manuel Lisa and the Spanish Fur Trade," *Southwest Historical Quarterly* 17 (July 1913); Richard Oglesby, *Manuel Lisa and the Opening of the Missouri Fur Trade* (Norman: University of Oklahoma Press, 1963), 134–35; letterbook of Comandante of N.M. to Comandante of Chihuahua, Santa Fe, November 20, 1814, no. 683, *SANM*, roll 17, frame 1088–89; *Missouri Gazette* (St. Louis), October 9, 1813, in Dale Morgan, comp., "The Mormons and the Far West," Beinicke Rare Book Library, Yale University.

10
See *Missouri Gazette*, July 29, 1815, and Morgan, "The Mormons and the Far West," in which Philibert describes Taos as "on the road to their former hunting camp," showing that the road was over the Sangre de Cristo Pass; Janet Lecompte, "Jules DeMun," in Hafen, ed., *Mountain Men and the Fur Trade*, 8: 97–104.

11
Alfred B. Thomas, ed., "Documents Bearing on the Northern Frontier of New Mexico, 1818–1819," *New Mexico Historical Review* 4 (April 1929). Thomas assumes that the Sierra Blanca meant the great massif Mount Blanca, as it does now, but in the eighteenth century Sierra Blanca meant the Raton Mountains, and in the early nineteenth century it meant the Sangre de Cristo Range.

12
A. B. Thomas, "An Anonymous Description of New Mexico, 1818," *Southwestern Historical Quarterly* 33 (July 1929): 54–56, 62; Elliott Coues, ed., *The Journal of Jacob Fowler: Narrating an Adventure from Arkansas through the Indian Territory, Oklahoma, Kansas, Colorado, and New Mexico, to*

the Sources of Rio Grande del Norte, 1821–22 (New York: Francis P. Harper, 1898), 98.

13
Becknell's journal in Archer Butler Hulbert, ed., Southwest on the Turquoise Trail: The First Diaries on the Road to Santa Fe, Overland to the Pacific Series (Colorado Springs: Stewart Commission of Colorado College, 1933), 2:62; The Historical Map of Las Animas County, Colorado, comp. Nancy Colvin Hirleman (La Veta, Colo.: 1982).

14
Max L. Moorhead, New Mexico's Royal Road: Trade and Travel on the Chihuahua Trail (Norman: University of Oklahoma Press, 1958).

15
David J. Weber, The Taos Trappers: The Fur Trade in the Far Southwest, 1540–1846 (Norman: University of Oklahoma Press, 1968).

16
Janet Lecompte, "Gantt's Fort and Bent's Picket Post," The Colorado Magazine 41 (Spring 1964): 111–25.

17
Louise Barry, The Beginning of the West: Annals of the Kansas Gateway to the American West, 1540–1854 (Topeka: Kansas State Historical Society, 1972), 276–77; Harold H. Dunham, "Charles Bent," in Mountain Men and the Fur Trade, 2:27–48. "Rio Colorado" could mean either the village near Questa, New Mexico, founded in 1815 at the western foot of the Sangre de Cristo Mountains or the Canadian River; Webb, Adventures in the Santa Fe Trade, 58–75, refers to both the settlement and the river of that name. For Charles Bent's store in Taos, see David Lavender, Bent's Fort (Garden City, N.Y.: Doubleday & Co., 1954), 145; for the store in Rio Colorado, see Albert D. Richardson, Beyond the Mississippi: From the Great River to the Great Ocean. Life and Adventure on the Prairies, Mountains, and Pacific Coast, 1857–1867 (Hartford, Conn.: American Publishing Co., 1867), 270; for Bent's wagons on the Sangre de Cristo Pass road, see Gwinn Harris Heap, Central Route to the Pacific: With Related Material on Railroad Explorations and Indian Affairs by Edward F. Beale, Thomas H. Benton, Kit Carson, and Col. E. A. Hitchcock, and in Other Documents, 1853–54, LeRoy R. Hafen and Ann W. Hafen, eds. (Glendale, Calif.: The Arthur H. Clark Company, 1957), 31.

18
Matt Field on the Santa Fe Trail, collected by Clyde and Mae Reed Porter and ed. John E. Sunder (Norman: University of Oklahoma Press, 1960), 160–63. This is the first reference I have found to the word Raton. Raton means mouse, but old-timers said it referred to gray squirrels peculiar to the Raton Mountains (George Simpson's testimony, Trinidad, Colorado, October 29, 1883, and Calvin Jones's testimony, Trinidad, October 31, 1883, Transcript of Record, The United States v. The Maxwell Land-Grant Company, U.S. Supreme Court, October term, 1886, no. 974).

19
Janet Lecompte, Pueblo, Hardscrabble, Greenhorn: The Upper Arkansas, 1832–1856 (Norman: University of Oklahoma Press, 1978), 70, 81, 88, 160–63.

20
Through the Country of the Comanche Indians in the Fall of the Year 1845: The Journal of a U.S. Army Expedition Led by Lieutenant James W. Abert of the Topographical Engineers, ed. John Galvin (San Francisco: John Howell Books, 1970), 13–14 and map opp. p. 130.

21
William Elsey Connelley, *Doniphan's Expedition and the Conquest of New Mexico and California* (Topeka: privately published, 1907), 185–86; John Galvin, ed., *Western America in 1846–1847: The Original Travel Diary of Lieutenant J. W. Abert Who Mapped New Mexico for the United States Army* (San Francisco: John Howell Books, 1966), 30; George Rutledge Gibson, *Journal of a Soldier under Kearny and Doniphan, 1846–1847*, ed. Ralph P. Bieber, *Southwest Historical Series* (Glendale, Calif.: The Arthur H. Clark Company, 1935), 60; Lewis H. Garrard, *Wah-to-Yah and the Taos Trail*, ed. Ralph P. Bieber, *Southwest Historical Series*, 6:313.

22
Down the Santa Fe Trail and into Mexico: The Diary of Susan Shelby Magoffin, 1846–1847, ed. Stella M. Drumm (New Haven: Yale University Press, 1926), 78–82.

23
"The Guadalupita Colony of Trinidad: A Posthumous Luis Baca Manuscript," *The Colorado Magazine* 21 (January 1944): 24; "Memoirs of Marian Russell," *The Colorado Magazine* 20 (September 1943): 195.

24
Conard, *"Uncle Dick" Wootton*, 418–19.

25
Ibid., 417–21.

26
Robert G. Athearn, *Rebel of the Rockies: A History of the Denver and Rio Grande Western Railroad* (New Haven and London: Yale University Press, 1962), 44, 92–94.

ESSAY SIX

Daniel D. Muldoon

Trappers and the Trail
The Santa Fe Trail from the Trapper's Perspective

About the author
Daniel D. Muldoon has been deeply involved in "historic living" research on the western beaver trappers since the early 1970s. He was a seasonal interpreter at Bent's Old Fort National Historic Site for five seasons and since 1984 has operated an 1839 Red River Trading Station living history site at the Museum of the Great Plains, Lawton, Oklahoma. He is on the board of directors of the Santa Fe Trail Council, the chief clerk and founding member of "The Opposition—A Company of Fur Trade Living Historians," and a member of the American Mountain Men.

SOON AFTER the Louisiana Purchase and the description of New Mexico by Zebulon M. Pike, Americans became increasingly interested in exploring the trade potential of the Southwest. Early attempts at commerce, however, were largely unsuccessful due to Spanish laws protecting the northern provinces from foreign trade.[1] With the imprisonment of the Baird-McKnight party in 1812[2] and the confiscation of $30,000 worth of goods and furs from the Chouteau-DeMun party in 1817, those inclined toward the western trade turned their attention away from New Spain and the Southwest.[3]

The Panic of 1819, however, gave Missouri merchants the incentive to look to the western prairies for commerce.[4] These merchants first began accepting more furs and then actively began seeking them through trade on the plains with either Indians or trappers.[5] One such trader-merchant was William Becknell, who, while seeking commerce with the Plains Indians, was in the right place at the right time in 1821 to take advantage of Mexico's new independence and the resulting relaxation of trade laws. Two other groups, the James and Glenn parties, came into Santa Fe shortly after Becknell, and while Becknell was the only one to find trade profitable, all three groups trapped beaver to some extent and Hugh Glenn returned to the United States with $5,000 worth of fur.

Americans quickly learned of the new situation, and large caravans soon began to travel the trail to New Mexico from towns in Missouri. Along with the usual dry goods, suitable for the New Mexican trade, these men also stocked goods that were necessary to the trappers who were now operating from bases in the northern Mexican towns. It was to the traders' advantage to take in beaver fur, since pelts were not taxed for export as was specie. Thus, for the next fifteen years beaver from the Southwest was a part of every returning caravan.[6] And since the Spanish had not utilized their fur resource at all, the Americans found the Southwest to be a virgin territory and quickly began to expand throughout it.[7]

From 1821 through 1824 trapping was not officially noticed by the Mexican government. In 1824 a law was passed restricting the Americans' activities, but it was not enforced until 1826.[8] The confiscation of furs was the chief threat to the trappers' business, so smuggling became the commonplace method used to avoid the Mexican authorities.[9] Rather than curtailing the practice of trapping in Mexico, however, this was a time of expansion, with parties moving as far west as the Pacific.[10]

Some parties did acquire the necessary licenses, either by taking along Mexican nationals, by using Mexican "front men" to apply for the licenses, or by taking out Mexican citizenship—as did James Baird, Mathew Kinkead, Charles Beaubien, William Wolfskill, James Kirker, and Ceran St. Vrain.[11] Regardless of whatever decrees were passed—aside from the threat of confiscation, which was generally avoided by smuggling[12]—the Mexican government, which had virtually no troops or horses to mount them,[13] could not enforce its laws.

The expansion of activities to the north met with the highly organized trapper brigades of General William Ashley,[14] while American trappers who reached California found that the Hudson's Bay Company was there first and in force.[15] This left the Gila and Colorado drainages for the southern trappers to exploit. In seeking new, untouched areas, trappers from New Mexico also attempted to operate in other regions, such as the Red River of north Texas, for which one large party left Picuris Pueblo in 1832.[16]

The concept of an annual rendezvous brought to the central Rockies by Ashley was not needed in the South, since Taos, Abiquiu, and Santa Fe were well established towns which had all the amenities, and American commerce provided both a supply of goods and a market for furs.[17] The trappers based in northern New Mexico were not usually the "indentured servant" type of company trapper. Most were of the "free trapper" class, but even they banded together into larger parties for mutual protection and a division of labor with a leader who enforced some form of organization and discipline.[18]

As the trappers utilized the northern New Mexican towns to rest and refit, they became familiar with the inhabitants and customs of the region, and this familiarity induced many to settle there either permanently or at least semipermanently. Another inducement for settlement was an increase in opportunities furnished these trappers by the American activity on the Santa Fe Trail, opportunities not available to the northern trappers except perhaps along the Columbia and Willamette rivers in Oregon. This diversity caused occupational distinctions to become blurred in New Mexico, with merchants becoming trappers, like George C. Yount, and trappers becoming merchants, like Jacob Leese.[19]

With New Mexico beyond the reach of the American trade and intercourse laws, the opportunity for the whiskey trade was opened as early as 1824 for some Americans: James Baird, Samuel Chambers, Thomas ("Peg-Leg") Smith (at this time yet with both legs), and a certain Stephens set up as distillers of "Taos Lightning."[20] Turley's Mill at Arroyo Hondo, a similar concern, offered employment to trappers such as Job Dye and Charles Autobees, who as a teetotaler was a dependable distributor of the product.[21]

Another nontrapping activity was initiated (or so James Ohio Pattie claimed) when James and Sylvester Pattie leased the Santa Rita copper mines in 1825.[22] By 1826 Robert McKnight was running the concern as a copper mine as well as a base of operations for trappers and as a cache to avoid the Mexican laws.[23] These mines also provided employment for some trappers, such as James Kirker, in escorting supply caravans from Chihuahua through Apache-held country.[24] A gruesome sideline which grew from this activity was scalphunting for the Mexican government, an occupation which attracted American trappers, adventurers, Shawnee Indians, and Mexicans in the employ of the Sonoran and Chihuahuan governments.[25]

The Santa Fe Trail also attracted some northern mountain men with its opportunities. In 1831 the partners Smith, Jackson and Sublette invested profits from the sale of their northern interests to the Rocky Mountain Fur Company in goods and headed southwest from Missouri. Smith, an early Ashley man and famous for his treks to California, was killed that year by Comanches along the Cimarron Cutoff; Sublette remained in New Mexico for a time but found the business and country not to his liking; and David Jackson initiated another twist to the possibilities by following a southern route to California on a mule-trading venture.[26]

In the mid-1830s, when hat-making technology improved and ways were found to substitute rabbit, raccoon, and, most importantly, nutria for beaver, the price of pelts declined drastically, putting many trappers at a disadvantage.[27] As the robe trade began to fill the void, many trappers turned to the newly constructed trading forts for employment. Bent, St. Vrain & Company's Fort William attracted many notable southern trappers such as John Smith, John Hatcher, Jean Baptiste Charbonneau, Thomas Boggs, Lucien Maxwell, and James P. Beckwourth, who were employed as traders, an occupation in which their knowledge and skills were put to good use.[28] Other trappers began their own small-scale trading ventures, outfitted partly with goods brought by way of the Santa

Fe Trail but also with the Taos whiskey produced by their fellow Americans in New Mexico.[29]

Pueblo de Leche (Milk Fort), six miles above Bent's Fort on the Arkansas, housed part-time traders and semiretired trappers, but it was short-lived, having been noted in 1839 but gone by 1841.[30] The forts on the South Platte outfitted on occasion via the Santa Fe Trail, with Lancaster P. Lupton passing by the Arkansas in 1839.[31] From 1843 until after the American conquest of New Mexico, Pueblo and its neighbors, Hardscrabble and Greenhorn, housed trapper-traders who joined with the regular caravans for mutual support and protection—though not always successfully, as Pueblo trader William Tharp was killed by Pawnees on the Santa Fe Trail in 1847.[32] Other traders farther to the west, such as Robidoux and Kirker, received goods by the Santa Fe Trail and caused much concern in New Mexico, for they traded weapons and ammunition to the Indians, allowing them to be better armed than the Mexicans.[33]

Along with trading, other fort-related employments attracted traders after the decline of beaver prices. Men like Kit Carson, Richens ("Uncle Dick") Wootton, Levin Mitchell, and Bill New were employed as hunters by Bent's Fort on occasion,[34] and as untrapperlike as it may seem, farming and stockraising occupied some. Hatcher and Boggs attempted to grow a crop of corn on the Ponil in New Mexico, and later Hatcher attempted to dig an irrigation ditch along the Purgatoire east of present Trinidad, Colorado, until trouble with the Utes drove him off.[35] Pueblo de Leche had an irrigated corn field in 1839,[36] and corn was raised at Pueblo, which troubled some traders along the Platte, for it was a much-sought trade item with the Indians and brought in many robes.[37]

With the increase in traffic on both the Santa Fe and Oregon trails, stockraising became profitable, though one of the first ventures in this area had nothing to do with work stock. Mathew Kinkead, the "Old Trapper" who sheltered Kit Carson during his first winter in Taos, acquired Mexican citizenship, land, and sheep and set up as a sheep rancher in New Mexico. As a result of Mexican hostility toward Anglos caused by Texas filibusters, he gave up his holdings and sent his sheep to Missouri. There they were traded for milk cows which were driven to the upper Arkansas and there used to raise captured buffalo calves; these, in turn, were eventually sent east along the Santa Fe Trail to be sold as curiosities in the States. Kinkead then invested the profits from this enterprise in trade goods and set up as a small-time trader on the site of Pueblo, Colorado.[38] Trappers used the Arkansas Valley to recruit stock traded on the Platte, where one good ox could be exchanged for two that were worn out. The trail also provided a market for California horseflesh stolen by trappers: a good number of the inhabitants of Pueblo during George F. Ruxton's 1847 visit had been participants in the 1839 horse raid to California from Fort Davy Crockett. This could explain the reason why so much of Ruxton's *Life in the Far West* is devoted to that activity.[39]

The Republic of Texas also offered trail-related employment to mountaineers when in 1843 Charles Warfield, a former trapper, began recruiting at the forts along the South Platte for a band of "volunteers" to wage war on the Mexican portions of the Santa Fe Trail caravans. He enlisted twenty-five men, among them Rufus Sage, and after failing to link up with a Texas-based unit under Jacob Snively, raided Mora, New Mexico, in May 1843. Five Mexicans were killed, four wounded, and eighteen taken prisoner but soon released. The Mexicans countered the success of this venture by capturing the party's horse herd, and the expedition returned on foot to the Arkansas River, where they were soon discharged.[40]

After the American conquest of New Mexico in 1846, many of the trappers' nontrapping activities, such as whiskey trading, became illegal; but with the discovery of gold in California in 1849 many of them, like James Kirker and John Gantt, found employment as guides for the Argonauts.[41] Others who had settled into New Mexican life remained there in one business or another, and some became involved in the early political life of the new territory. Charles Bent, for example, became the first territorial governor, Wootton became sheriff of Taos, Levin Mitchell deputy sheriff, and Thomas Fitzpatrick Indian agent with his headquarters for the Upper Arkansas Agency at Bent's Fort.[42]

The Santa Fe Trail provided an opportunity for trappers to operate successfully and brought an increase in options for trappers once fur prices dropped. The trappers, in return, gave the trail's merchants manpower for the caravans along with customers and a much-sought commodity. The history of both the fur trade of the Southwest and the Santa Fe Trail are deeply linked.

1
Paul Chrisler Phillips, *The Fur Trade*, 2 vols. (Norman: University of Oklahoma Press, 1961) 2:53.

2
David J. Weber, *The Taos Trappers: The Fur Trade in the Far Southwest, 1540–1846* (Norman: University of Oklahoma Press, 1971), 44.

3
Phillips, *Fur Trade*, 2:507–8; Weber, *Taos Trappers*, 53–56.

4
David J. Weber, *The Mexican Frontier* (Albuquerque: University of New Mexico Press, 1982), 125.

5
Weber, *Taos Trappers*, 53–56.

6
Ibid., 56

7
Phillips, *Fur Trade*, 2:492–93; Weber, *Taos Trappers*, 67–70.

8
Phillips, *Fur Trade*, 2:516–17; Weber, *Taos Trappers*, 66–67.

9
Weber, *Taos Trappers*, 127.

10
Phillips, *Fur Trade*, 2:552.

11
Weber, *Taos Trappers*, 176–88.

12
Ibid., 133.

13
Ibid., 114–15.

14
Phillips, *Fur Trade*, 2:515.

15
Ibid., 553; Weber, *Taos Trappers*, 152.

16
Albert Pike, "Narrative of a Journey in the Prairie," *Panhandle Plains Historical Review* 41 (1969) ed. J. Evetts Haley, 1–84.

17
David Lavender, *Bent's Fort* (Garden City, N.Y.: Doubleday & Co., 1954; Lincoln and London: University of Nebraska Press, 1972), 62; Phillips, *Fur Trade*, 512; Weber, *Taos Trappers*, 9.

18
Iris Higbie Wilson, *William Wolfskill, 1798–1866: Frontier Trapper to California Rancher* (Glendale, Calif.: The Arthur H. Clark Company, 1965), 66–71.

19
Charles L. Camp, "George C. Yount," in LeRoy R. Hafen, ed., *Mountain Men and the Fur Trade of the Far West*, 10 vols. (Glendale, Calif.: The Arthur H. Clark Company, 1969), 9:411–20; Gloria G. Cline, "Jacob Leese," *Mountain Men and the Fur Trade*, 3:189–96.

20
Weber, *Taos Trappers*, 72.

21
Gloria G. Cline, "Job Dye," *Mountain Men and the Fur Trade*, 1:259–71; Janet Lecompte, "Charles Autobees," *Mountain Men and the Fur Trade*, 4:21–37.

22
The Personal Narrative of James O. Pattie (Lincoln and London: University of Nebraska Press, 1984), 74.

23
William Cochran McGaw, *Savage Scene* (New York: Hastings House, 1972), 76–77; Weber, *Taos Trappers*, 143.

24
McGaw, *Savage Scene*, 87.

25
Ibid., 120–37.

26
See the following in *Mountain Men and the Fur Trade:* Harvey L. Carter, "Jedediah Smith," 8:331–48, Carl D. W. Hays, "David Jackson," 9:215–44, and John E. Sunder, "William Sublette," 5:347–59.

27
Charles E. Hanson, Jr., "The Nutria and the Beaver Hat," *Museum of the Fur Trade Quarterly* 12 (Fall 1976): 6–10.

28
Janet Lecompte, *Pueblo, Hardscrabble, Greenhorn* (Norman: University of Oklahoma Press, 1978), 20; Lavender, *Bent's Fort*, 155, 223–24.

29
Phillips, *Fur Trade*, 2:533; Lecompte, *Pueblo, Hardscrabble, Greenhorn*, 18, 87.

30
Lecompte, *Pueblo, Hardscrabble, Greenhorn*, 18.

31
Ann W. Hafen, "Lancaster P. Lupton," *Mountain Men and the Fur Trade*, 2:211.

32
Lecompte, *Pueblo, Hardscrabble, Greenhorn*, 200–201.

33
Weber, *Taos Trappers*, 222.

34
Lavender, *Bent's Fort*, 199.

35
Ibid., 263; Lecompte, *Pueblo, Hardscrabble, Greenhorn*, 199.

36
Lecompte, *Pueblo, Hardscrabble, Greenhorn*, 18.

37
Ibid., 170–71.

38
Ibid., 36–40

39
George Frederick Ruxton, *Life in the Far West*, ed. LeRoy R. Hafen (Norman: University of Oklahoma Press, 1979), chaps. 6, 7.

40
Nicholas P. Hardeman, "Charles Warfield," *Mountain Men and the Fur Trade*, 7:353–63.

41
McGaw, *Savage Scene*, 194; Harvey L. Carter, "John Gantt," *Mountain Men and the Fur Trade*, 5:101–15.

42
Lavender, *Bent's Fort*, 289; see also the following in *Mountain Men and the Fur Trade:* Harold H. Dunham, "Charles Bent: 2:27–48, Harvey L. Carter, "Dick Wootton" 3:397–411, Janet Lecompte, "Levin Mitchell" 5:239–47.

ESSAY SEVEN

David A. Sandoval

Who Is Riding the Burro Now?
A Bibliographical Critique of Scholarship on the New Mexican Trader

About the author
David A. Sandoval holds his M.A. from Southern Methodist University and his Ph.D. from the University of Utah. He received a 1986 NEH postdoctoral grant to study with David Weber at Southern Methodist University. Presently a professor of Chicano Studies/History at the University of Southern Colorado, Sandoval has taught in the Denver Public Schools, Metropolitan State College, University of Utah, Eastern New Mexico University, and the University of Colorado at Boulder.

Essays and Monographs

You might say that the American government is like a burro, but on this burro jog along the lawyers and not the clergy.—*Antonio José Martínez to his students, September, 1846*[1]

BY 1843 Mexican merchants dominated the Santa Fe trading system, yet most historical literature about the Santa Fe Trail has relegated these entrepreneurs to a subordinate position. This essay explores how and why *nuevomejicanos* on the Santa Fe–Missouri segment of the trail have commanded less-than-adequate attention. An exploration of nineteenth-century glimpses of New Mexican merchants and new directions for interpretation may help to fill this large gap in our understanding of trail historiography.

Historians face a number of challenges in trying to explain the role of New Mexicans in the Santa Fe trade. Besides the matter of interpretation, there are questions of definition, perspective, and scope—issues that are finally being addressed by scholars who are working in Spanish-language sources. Max Moorhead in *New Mexico's Royal Road* convincingly defines the scope of the trading system. The Santa Fe Trail, he suggests, is a misnomer; rather, he regards Santa Fe as the hub of a commercial enterprise with transcontinental spokes. His book is by far the most complete analysis of the system.[2] In addition, David Weber asserts that New Mexicans should be considered in the contextual light of a northern Mexican borderland.[3] And Jack Rittenhouse's most valuable bibliographical tool contains an understandable parameter in the statement that "to include everything would be to compile a bibliography of the entire West and much of the South."[4] A common element shared by these historians is that they recognize the need for more research dealing with the trail from the Mexican perspective and seem to reject the claim that any present study or series of studies can be regarded as definitive.

Nineteenth-century Anglo-American observers of the Santa Fe Trail and its trade reflect the opinions of their time, interest, and social class, all of which occasionally tainted their periodic glimpses of their Mexican counterparts and competitors in the Santa Fe trade. Thus the grist of nineteenth-century opinion available for twentieth-century historians is mixed with nativism, ethnocentrism, expansionism, personalism, nationalism, and racism. The number of works that dissect those contemporary attitudes should sound sufficient warning that many Anglos on the Santa Fe Trail were less than kind to Mexicans who left footprints in the Kansas dust.[5]

George Sibley, who traveled the trail in 1825 in an official capacity to mark a governmentally approved and protected route, probably shared the impressions of many others who began to reap the profits of the lucrative intercourse when, before actually setting out to that "miserable spot," he wrote about the New Mexicans. His preconceived notion that the country lacked development due to a New Mexican "want of enterprise and industry" was probably not altered by his personal experience. He eschewed a racial condemnation of the New Mexicans for being "poor and ignorant" as he thought that they lacked sufficient time to have recovered from Spain's colonial rule. Apparently believing the New Mexicans not biologically inferior, as they were "fast improving in liberal principles," he remained concerned at the New Mexican bias "against the proper encouragement of a liberal intercourse with our people."

The diaries of three American surveyors, Sibley, Joseph Davis, and Benjamin Reeves, are silent regarding Mexican traders in New Mexico or on the trail in 1825 and 1826 but they share similar observations of later travelers in their ethnocentricity. At a campsite which they named "Louse Camp Creek" they confidently asserted that the discovery of body lice confirmed their belief "that the camp had been occupied by Spaniards." Sibley may not have known of the twenty-six New Mexicans who traveled to Council Bluffs that same year in order to encourage trade and entreat with the Pawnees for the protection of the trade.[6]

Observers on officially sanctioned expeditions commented most often through vested-interest lobbying efforts during the 1820s. As such, many of the early accounts are preserved in official records.[7] In addition, the newspapers began to include some accounts that would lead to a plethora of comments, fascination with the exotic, and eventually to a style of literature. The *Missouri Intelligencer* published an early, somewhat humorous, American account on August 19, 1825:

> The Book of the Muleteers
>
> 5. And he said there lieth over against us a province wherein dwelleth a people called Montezumians.
>
> 6. And they go in and out of tabernacles of clay and they be miners and shepherds.

7. And they have among them gold and silver and precious furs and ass colts in abundance and they be moreover a barbarous people and heathen idolators.

Chapter II

7. . . . and lo! a people came forth from their tabernacles of clay and their skin was like the skin of Ethiope.[8]

At this time, New Mexicans were apparently not viewed as equals or even as possible competitors.

The development of a New Mexican merchant class, with all of its implications, does seem rather remarkable, especially given the level of economic development of the province in 1821. Chihauhua merchants had dominated commerce into New Mexico during the latter portion of the eighteenth century, and in the census of 1790 the only merchants in New Mexico consisted of Don José Mariano de la Pena, a thirty-one-year-old single native of Mexico City living with three servants in San Ysidro de Paxarito, and Don José Rafael Sarracino, a native of the town of Chihuahua who also had a home in Santa Fe.[9] Moorhead identifies some of the Chihuahua merchants who controlled commerce at the time of independence through governmental sanction.[10]

The incomplete 1823 census recorded Don Esteban Pino, a merchant in Santa Fe with his two sons, Don Manuel and Don Justo, students who would master the commercial trade. Don Atancio Volivar is reported to be a merchant as well as Don José Francisco Baca, who married Doña Dolores Ortiz.[11] Rámon García and Manuel Símon de Escudero were probably two Chihuahua merchants on the trail in 1826.[12] This group also included a *fiador* (agent), Don Salvador Martín del Bado, and two others, Don José Cavallero and Nestor Armijo.[13]

The decade of the 1820s witnessed the saturation of the market in New Mexico, the introduction of wagons and oxen, the expansion of the southern trade, and the embryonic development of a New Mexican merchant class. Local officials encouraged the Anglo-American traders, participated in the commerce, and began to look for additional markets. New occupations became available, basic necessities as well as luxuries were at hand, and the New Mexicans expanded out of the Rio Grande Valley into the northern Pecos River region, marking the trail with their homes and lives.

The decade of the 1830s heralded an increased New Mexican involvement in commerce. Partnerships were apparently formed with Chihuahuan merchants as well as Anglo-Americans, but, unfortunately, very few *nuevomejicanos* garnered descriptions from Anglo-Americans. By examining the *guías* (passports) preserved in the Mexican Archives of New Mexico, one becomes overwhelmed by the number of New Mexicans involved in the southern route between Santa Fe and Chihuahua; many of these merchants were also involved in the trade to the United States. A mid-decade list of almost 100 owners on the southern route reveals that nearly 75 percent were New Mexicans.[14] Of ten owners in the July 1836 group, six New Mexicans as well as Santiago Abreu with "Yentry Floid" apparently paid taxes.[15] In December of that year customs officials recorded merchants and agents as well as their ports of entry, which probably indicated their homes instead of actual entry areas.[16] United States merchants such as Josiah Gregg, Manuel Alvarez, and Charles Bent often complained of unfair treatment and inherent advantages of New Mexican merchants, which included the ability to store goods in their homes and thereby reduce the costs of conducting business.

Beyond official and unofficial complaints concerning "unfair" advantages, New Mexicans seldom were recorded by name by the writers of the day. For example, newspaperman Matt Field on his first journey in 1839 included a New Mexican merchant whom he misnamed [Don Antonio José Luna], but this regular contributor to the *New Orleans Picayune* used common practices and simply referred to "Mexican" traders. The singular exception remains "José David" [Don Antonio José Chávez].[17]

The Mexican Archives of New Mexico, combined with periodic contemporary glimpses, may help resolve speculation concerning past assumptions—for example, whether or not the Rio Abajo area provided the majority of merchants. This generation saw capital consolidation and expansion of opportunities not only for baronial families but for *arreiros* (muleteers), *fiadores*, translators, and numerous other New Mexicans who took advantage of economic opportunities to trade in and beyond the Mexican interior, in California, and in the United States, particularly in St. Louis, Philadelphia, and New York. When one begins to list all of the participants involved in the trade in all directions, the magnitude of New Mexican involvement becomes apparent. The "Montezumians" certainly merit an accurate account from the historian writing about the Santa Fe Trail or New Mexico during the Mexican period.

Contemporary writers such as James Pattie, George Kendall, Manuel Alvarez, Susan Magoffin, Lewis Garrard, Josiah Gregg, James Webb, Albert Pike, Alphonso Wetmore, Augustus Storrs, and Matt Field, although often jaundiced as well as biased in their treatment of the New Mexicans, do allow a peek at the New Mexican merchant from time to time. Josiah Gregg speaks well, once, of a specific New Mexican merchant and suggests, at the same time, the level of New Mexican involvement in the Santa Fe trade.

> In 1843, the greater portion of the traders were New Mexicans . . . Don Mariano Chavez . . . gentleman of very amiable character, such as is rarely to be met with in that unfortunate land. It is asserted that he furnished a considerable quantity of provisions, blankets, etc., to Col. Cooke's division of Texan prisoners.[18]

Don Mariano José Chávez must have truly been a gentleman from any land considering the murder of his brother and invasion of his homeland. Antonio José Chávez was tortured and robbed by the John and David McDaniel gang purporting to be part of the Texas army. Whether or not Don Mariano bore a grudge after the 1843 murder has not been consistently addressed by historians; in any event, the power of the Chávez family proved sufficient to result in the execution of two of the raiders.

Matthew Field and Benjamin Hayes also had occasional kind comments about the New Mexicans,[19] but most writers expressed themselves as did Charles Bent, with his broken spelling, in 1846:

> They are not fit to be free, they should be ruled by others than themselves. Mexico has tryed long enough to prove to the world that she is not able to govern herself, whare thar is no morality, honesty, or Patriotesim of caracter that people ar not fit for self-government. . . . They are corrupt, destitute of all principal, lasy indolent ignorant and base to the last degree. . . . They think themselves superior to all the world. . . . The Mexican caracter is made up of stupidity, Obstanacy, Ignorance duplicity and vanity.[20]

Who Is Riding the Burro Now?

In the eighteen years that passed between Sibley's observation of the "ignorant" New Mexicans and Philip St. George Cooke's 1843 protective escort, the *nuevomejicanos* achieved dominance of the trade. Cooke reported that within the July caravan, ten American owners and five Mexican owners possessed more than 56 wagons. He noted that Mexicans owned 32 of the wagons. When he encountered the September caravan of 140 wagons, he observed that all had Mexican owners. However, he wrote that rains caused the "overloaded and ill managed wagon train" to move slowly. He also named two of the New Mexican merchants, Armijo and Ortiz, within that protected July caravan. Fascinated by Ortiz's skill at lancing a buffalo cow at full speed riding bareback, Cooke recalled this "very small man" and his exploits.[21] Juan Nepomenceno Gutierres, José Chaves y Castillo, and Juan A. Gutierres traveled in that expedition but the identity of Cooke's "Ortiz" is not certain. Perhaps it was Gaspar Ortis or Francisco Ortis y Delgado, as they also conveyed wares with this group.[22] The latter caravan, principally owned by Tomás Gonzales, Jośe Mariano Gutierrez, Antonio Sandoval, Mariano Chávez, and Rafael Armijo, probably included Anglo-Americans despite Cooke's observations, as the New Mexicans traveled slowly and others joined them according to information available through New Mexican tax records.[23]

The so-called "ignorant" Montezumians from Gregg's "unfortunate land," portrayed as pretentious, stupid people by Bent, do not seem to be the same souls who emerge from the U. S. House of Representatives Committee of Claims report which addressed damages incurred by New Mexican traders in 1846. When threatened with alternative routes, the New Mexicans had flexed their political muscle and assured themselves control of the trade through the Mexican government as early as 1839. Their continued obvious political sophistication in international business and political circles is evident in Manuel X. Harmony's successful claim for damages when numerous wares for which he was the agent became casualties of the war with Mexico. Harmony lodged a claim for over $100,000 and the Committee of Claims reported in his favor "a bill for the relief of the petitioner."[24]

Perhaps historians and social scientists have begun to "uncover a past long ignored by academics"[25] and not a little oversimplified through "the omission of critical cultural, geographical or political factors."[27] Janet Lecompte's observation of the propagandist use of "exaggeration, generalizations, unfounded assumptions, untruths, and an occasional nugget of pure and undeniable fact" can be applied beyond the "new" social histories in many ways.[27] Thankfully, scholars who have recently worked in various archival repositories have delivered coherent bibliographies, guides, and finding aids basic to the historian's research.[28] Perhaps the quality of their research and the obvious need to consult their literature will temper the polemicist by providing details to buttress theory.[29]

Many new interpretations rely heavily on territorial period literature. The works by Lansing Bloom in *Old Santa Fe*, H. H. Bancroft's *History of Arizona and New Mexico* (San Francisco: History Co., 1889), Ralph Twitchell's 1909 *History of the Military Occupation of the Territory of New Mexico from 1846 to 1851 by the Government of the United States* (Chicago: Rio Grande Press, 1963), Francisco de Thoma's 1896 *Historia popular de Neuvo México*, and Paul A. F. Walter's testimonial biography *Colonel José Francisco Chávez* seem the materials most heavily relied on to describe New Mexican merchants.

Francisco de Thoma's publication is particularly interesting when compared to Twitchell's.[30] While the scope of these works is different, it is interesting to compare these contemporaries in their treatment of New Mexicans, particularly in their discussion of conspirators in the events of December 1846. The object of this conspiracy was the removal of American forces, and the role of the New Mexican *rico* is often portrayed as a collaboration. The specific identification of persons, especially merchants, however, contradicts that judgment. The two lists of conspirators in these works differ significantly. Twitchell includes residents of Taos and may have been influenced by the politics of his own era. He certainly deals with several of the political factions at a time of pronounced conflict during the territorial period. De Thoma relies on Bancroft and had the assistance of Don Amado Chávez as well as the scrutiny of church officials J. B. Salpointe and P. L. Chapelle, but both writers make obvious errors. For example, De Thoma follows Bancroft's lead and identifies Don Jose Antonio Baca as the trail blazer for "el comercio con California" and Twitchell calls the famous Tules "Barcelona." Obviously the conduct of New Mexican oligarchs on the Santa Fe Trail and during the war consisted of complex relationships and should be based on more reliable sources.

Beyond simple identification, any attempt to understand the nature of the New Mexican merchants becomes more difficult by the continuous repetition of stories that belong to a different era.[31] Historical accounts for almost a hundred years after the conquest differ very little from earlier accounts. The territorial period demanded a *realpolitik* perspective, and some New Mexican merchants appeared in print. Perhaps those who were ignored did not conform to a partisan publisher's view of proper politics. Occasionally a view of the New Mexican surfaced through the publication of a work like *Three New Mexican Chronicles*, in 1942, an exception to a legacy of misunderstanding.[32]

Be that as it may, the treatment of Mexican merchants is usually expressed as Robert L. Duffus did in 1930 in *The Santa Fe Trail* (Albuquerque: University of New Mexico Press, 1930). Duffus recognizes that "by the early forties half the trade was in Mexican hands" (p. 134). In spite of this, he also asserts that "Americans [were] so strong that the traders of Chihuahua and the south of Mexico could less than ever compete with them" (p. 106). He does capture the ethnocentrism of the 1840s with a 1930s flavor as he describes the "brown children, tumbling out of the adobe houses" and the "Mexican girls with more than half an eye for the *Americanos;* and here are sleepy, lounging Mexican men, half-resentful, half-friendly" (p. 97).

A similar dismissal of the New Mexican trader can be found in the more recent work by Seymour V. Connor and Jimmy M. Skaggs entitled *Broadcloth and Britches: The Santa Fe Trade* (College Station: Texas A&M University Press, 1977), who draw a picture of the Santa Fe trade on the eve of the war by abstracting from contemporary newspapers. These abstracts hint at Mexican participation; for example, the *Jefferson Inquirer* of March 21, 1846, notes the arrival of an Armijo in Independence after being robbed by the Pawnees and following a 200-mile walk, and the *Missouri Reporter* notes that a "Spanish" company consisting of A. [Ambrosio?] Armijo, James Florris [Flores], and Mr. Lussard are on their way to purchase goods in New York (p. 122). Even with that glimpse, however, this "new" work ignores the Mexican merchant. In sum, Henry Inman's 1891 history of the trail, Robert Duffus's 1930 treatment, and the more recent work by Connor and Skaggs are all interesting but incomplete publications concerning the Santa Fe Trail. One cannot extol the magnificence of Max Moorhead's work too much as it is made even more significant by perfunctory treatments.

Periodically, the expressed desire to deal more adequately with New Mexican merchants is realized. In 1944 Albert Bork attempted, in "Nuevos aspectos de comercio entre Nuevo México y Misurí, 1822–1846" (Ph.D. diss.: Universidad Nacional Autonoma de Mexico, 1944), to treat Mexican traders. Bork, however, tantalizes the reader with items that raise additional questions. For example, while listing conspirators in a plot to assassinate Governor Manuel Armijo, he identifies a member of the prominent Sarracino trading family as a *judio* (Jew). Given the experience of the Spanish Inquisition, one can only wonder if this might be a pejorative label. Similarly, Carolyn Zeleny, in her *Relations between the Spanish-Americans and Anglo Americans in New Mexico* (New York: Arno Press, 1974), which is based on her 1944 dissertation, speculates that "the mores of the group [New Mexicans] included the extension of such favors as the Mexican women thought fit to bestow upon the American traders under the heading of hospitality, and that little trouble was caused by it."

A legacy of misunderstanding based on ethnocentric perceptions followed by a legion of competing interpretations confuse the effort to find a clear sense of the New Mexican merchant. Yet, even though much of the newest literature fails to consider time sequence, geography, or regional differences, the more recent theoretical works have had the beneficial effect of bringing new information to light.[33] Ángela Moyano Pahissa in *El comercio de Santa Fe y la Guerra del '47* (Mexico: Secretaria de Educacion Publica, 1976) and Gilberto López y Rívas in *La Guerra del '47 y la resistencia popular á la ocupación* (Mexico City: Nuestro Tiempo, 1976) seem more interested in an accumulation of details that fit a Marxist interpretation of the trade than the trade itself. Moyano Pahissa even attributes the 1837 Chimayo rebellion to "norteamericanos," presumably merchants; while López y Rívas's contribution may be more than his interesting bibliography. Most modern historians reject the thesis that Anglo-Americans were involved in the 1837 rebellion against Governor Albino Pérez, and Janet Lecompte's recent publication concerning this rebellion should bury the matter once and for all. Nevertheless, these two works seem to be more complete than the Inman, Duffus, or Connor and Skaggs contributions.

Beyond works that examine the specific nature of the Santa Fe trail, many others touch upon the New Mexican merchants as well as the role of the route in binational histories. New Mexicans have not escaped the wrath of ethnohistorians like Rodolfo Acuña, who wrote that "the reality that a small oligarchy of Anglo Americans, aided by a small group of 'ricos' established their privilege at the expense of the Mexican masses has been conveniently ignored."[34] Unfortunately, Acuña relies heavily on those same references that he castigates so vehemently. In his desire to destroy the so-called "fantasy" heritage, Acuña maintains that New Mexican merchants betrayed their country and their people. Matt S. Meier and Feliciano Rivera also seem to ignore *nuevomejicano* merchant resistance to the conquest of New Mexico as they assert in *The Chicanos: A History of Mexican Americans* (New York: Hill and Wang, 1972) that "from the very beginning of the American period many New Mexican landowners and merchants, often referred to as 'ricos,' welcomed Anglo take-over and control" (p. 96). This reliance on twentieth-century values and standards, based on misinformation and incomplete studies, to judge a society over 100 years ago seems absurd. The indictment of New Mexican merchants should be substantiated with concrete proof if evidence exists.[35]

Paul Horgan's prize-winning *Great River*, more typical of monographic treatments of New Mexicans, simply ignores the New Mexican traders. Howard Lamar's *Far Southwest* is almost two paragraphs better than Horgan, and David Weber's *Mexican Frontier* devotes almost three pages to the Santa Fe trade, albeit mostly devoted to the Anglo-American merchants.[36]

Internal colonialism theories, the development of world capitalism, and the role of religion as a capitalistic tool may lead to historical explanations of causation as explained through the frontier process. These analyses will be of use if in the process archival sources are translated and preserved. Through those pursuits a greater understanding of the region becomes possible. Before the jury comes back, however, we should at least know more of the people.

Be that as it may, delightful exceptions to theoretical musings that portend substantive contributions emerge among some employing different techniques and disciplines. Contributing scholars include: W. H. Timmons, John O. Baxter, Ruth Armstrong, Marc Simmons, Daniel Tyler, Janet Lecompte, Ward Alan Minge, Lynn Perrigo, David Weber, Richard Nostrand, Oakah Jones, and Frances Leon Swadesh as well as Alicia J. Tjarks, Fray Angelico Chavez,

Richard Salazar, and Virginia Olmstead.[37] Some of these individuals have utilized the Turnerian frontier thesis, from the Mexican perspective, to explain the development of societal institutions.

In summary, biased historical accounts read in the light of turn-of-the-century attitudes have drawn jaded portraits of the New Mexican merchants. When Governor Manuel Armijo issued his proclamation asking for the defense of New Mexico, he stated that "if we are not able to preserve the integrity of our Territory, all this country would very soon be the prey of the greed and enterprising spirit of our neighbors on the north, and nothing would remain save a sad remembrance of our political existence." An examination of the treatment of New Mexican merchants in the years that have passed reveals worse than a "sad remembrance"—with few exceptions there has been *no* remembrance. Lost in a shuffle, *nuevomejicano* merchants have most recently been perceived as a component within the global village by social science historiography. As such, stereotypes persist and few writers have used their talents to draw new portraits with their articles, monographs, or textual contributions. In the midst of new theoretical works, New Mexico has attracted scholars who prepare the fields for a bountiful harvest. The present need is for those who would bring in the crops, even if that requires plowing under established interpretations.

1. Lansing B. Bloom, *Old Santa Fe* 2 (April 1915): 379. Father Martinez here insightfully captures one of the significant changes in this society. The perspective of this essay is concerned with the treatment and portrayal of New Mexican merchants by both contemporaries and historians. In most instances, New Mexicans are slighted or ignored. One has to wonder if writers will ever afford them a burro to ride, a wagon to guide, or a mosquito to swat along the Santa Fe Trail.

2. Max L. Moorhead, *New Mexico's Royal Road: Trade and Travel on the Chihuahua Trail* (Norman: University of Oklahoma Press, 1958).

3. Weber points to the paucity of biographies in "Mexico's Far Northern Frontier, 1821–1854: Historiography Askew," *Western Historical Quarterly* 7 (July 1976): 279–93. See also David J. Weber, "Turner, the Boltonians, and the Borderlands," *American Historical Review* 91 (February 1986): 66–81, and his *The Mexican Frontier, 1821–1846: The American Southwest under Mexico* (Albuquerque: University of New Mexico Press, 1982).

4. Jack D. Rittenhouse, *The Santa Fe Trail: A Historical Bibliography* (Albuquerque: University of New Mexico Press, 1971), 28.

5. See, for example, John P. Bloom, "New Mexico Viewed by Anglo Americans, 1846–1849," *New Mexico Historical Review* [hereafter *NMHR*] 34 (July 1959): 165–98. Raymund A. Paredes, in "The Mexican Image in American Travel Literature, 1831–1869," *NMHR* 52 (January 1977): 139–65, emphasizes James Pattie, Josiah Gregg, George W. Kendall, and Albert Pike. His most obvious omission is the writings of Matt Field, who regularly published in the *New Orleans Picayune* and whose works have been edited by John E. Sunder, *Matt Field on the Santa Fe Trail* (Norman: University of Oklahoma Press, 1960). See also Doris L. Meyer, "Early Mexican American Responses to Negative Stereotyping," *NMHR* 53 (January 1978): 75–91; Burl Noggle, "Anglo Observers of the Southwest Borderlands, 1825–1890: The Rise of a Concept," *Arizona and the West* 1 (Summer 1959): 105–41; David J. Weber, "'Scarce More than Apes'": Historical Roots of Anglo American Stereotypes of Mexicans in the Border Region," 293–307, in *New Spain's Far Northern Frontier: Essays on Spain in the American West, 1540–1821* (Albuquerque: University of New Mexico Press, 1979); Philip W. Powell, *"Tree of Hate": Propaganda and Prejudices Affecting United States Relations with the Hispanic World* (New York: Basic Books, 1971); Cecil Robinson, *Mexico and the Hispanic Southwest in American Literature* (Tucson: University of Arizona Press, 1977); Reginald Horsman, *Race and Manifest Destiny: The Origins of American Racial Anglo-Saxonism* (Cambridge: Harvard University Press, 1977); and Sandra L. Myres, "Mexican American and Westering Anglos: A Feminine Perspective," *NMHR* 57 (October 1982): 317–34.

6. Kate Gregg, in *The Road to Santa Fe* (Albuquerque: University of New Mexico, 1952), sets George C. Sibley and others in the context of their time and adds an extensive scholarly analysis.

7. Thomas Hart Benton, "Statement on Trade between Missouri and Mexico," January 3, 1825, *Senate Documents*, Vol. 1, No. 7, 18th Cong. 2d

sess.; Inhabitants of Missouri, "Petition on Communications with Mexico," October 1824, *Executive Papers*, Vol. 4, No. 79, 18th Cong., 2d sess.; "Statement on Intercourse between Missouri and Mexico," November 1824, *Senate Documents*, Vol. 1, No. 7, 18th Cong., 2d sess.

8
Arthur Woodward, "Adventuring to Santa Fe," *NMHR* 17 (October 1942): 289–91.

9
Virginia Olmstead, *New Mexico Spanish and Mexican Colonial Censuses: 1790, 1823, 1845* (Albuquerque: New Mexico Genealogical Society, 1975), 25, 53. There are eight muleteers listed.

10
Moorhead, *Royal Road*, 53–54.

11
Olmstead, *New Mexico Censuses*, 140.

12
Mexican Archives of New Mexico (hereafter MANM), reel 6, frame 464, *guia* 10 to Ramon Garcia; David A. Sandoval, "Trade and the *Manito* Society in New Mexico, 1821–1848" (Ph.D. diss., University of Utah, 1978), 94–95. Ramon Garcia was reported robbed on the trail in 1823 and a "Spaniard" had been killed by the Pawnees in 1823. Andrew Jackson, "Message on the Fur Trade and Trade to Mexico," February 9, 1838, *Senate Documents*, Vol. 2, No. 90, 22d Cong., 1st sess.; Alphonso Wetmore's diary is also included in this selection.

13
MANM, reel 6, frame 299.

14
Ibid., reel 21, frames 272–92.

15
Ibid., reel 22, frame 1121.

16
Ibid., reel 22, frames 1211–13.

17
Sunder, ed., *Matt Field* xxiv.

18
Josiah Gregg, *Commerce of the Prairies*, ed. Max L. Moorhead (Norman: University of Oklahoma Press, 1954), 333, 341.

19
Marjorie T. Wolcott, ed., "Pioneer Notes from the Diaries of Judge Benjamin L. Hayes," cited by John Bloom in "New Mexico Viewed by Anglo Americans," 183, as "polite, kind, mild, well-meaning people, respecting the laws, and eminently religious in their feelings. 'Tis a contracted pedant who would blame them for their want of education."

20
Frank D. Reeve, ed., "Charles Bent Papers, 1837–1846," *NMHR* 30 (July 1955): 254. David Lavender assures us that this quotation was atypical of Bent's attitude. See *Bent's Fort* (Garden City, N.Y.: Doubleday & Co., 1954; Lincoln: University of Nebraska Press, 1972). The reader should glance at the series of papers edited by Reeve in *NMHR* from July 1954 to July 1956 and decide whether or not this quotation was atypical.

21
William E. Connelley, ed., "Documents, A Journal of the Santa Fe Trail," *Mississippi Valley Historical Review* 12 (June 1925–March 1926): 98, 240, 241, 250.

22
MANM, reel 34, frames 1166, 1176, 1179, 1180, 1182.

23
Ibid., reel 34, frames 1171, 1190, 1191, 1193, 1198.

24
House Reports, 30th Cong., 1st sess., Vol. 21, March 30, 1848, Report 458,

to accompany H. R. 388, pp. 1–63; *House Reports*, 30th Cong., 1st sess., Report 458, "Manuel X. Harmony," March 21, 1848, letter from Mc. C. Young, acting secretary of the treasury, to Hon. John A. Rockwell, chairman of committee of claims; *Despatches from United States Consuls in Santa Fe, 1830–1846* (Washington: National Archives and Records Center, No. 199, 1951); "Insurrection against the Military Government in New Mexico and California, 1847 and 1848," June 5, 1900, *Senate Documents*, 56th Cong., 1st sess., Report 442.

25
Albert Camarillo, "Perspectives on Mexican-American Urban Life and Culture," *Journal of American Ethnic History* 5 (Spring 1986).

26
Lawrence R. Murphy's book review of Roxanne Ortiz Dunbar's *Roots of Resistance: Land Tenure in New Mexico*, in *NMHR* 57 (January 1982): 90.

27
Janet Lecompte, "Manuel Armijo's Family History," *NMHR* 48 (July 1973): 54.

28
Cheryl J. Foote, "Selected Sources for the Mexican Period, 1821–1848, in New Mexico," *NMHR* 59 (January 1984): 81–89; Thomas C. Barnes, Thomas H. Naylor, and Charles W. Polzer, *Northern New Spain: A Research Guide* (Tucson: University of Arizona Press, 1981); Frances Leon Swadesh, *20,000 Years of History: A New Mexico Bibliography* (Santa Fe: Sunstone Press, 1973); Richard E. Greenleaf and Michael C. Meyer, *Research in Mexican History: Topics, Methodology, Sources. A Practical Guide to Field Research* (Lincoln: University of Nebraska Press, 1973); Myra Ellen Jenkins, *Calendar of the Mexican Archives of New Mexico, 1821–1846* (Santa Fe: State of New Mexico Records Center, 1970); Fray Angelico Chavez, *Archives of the Archdiocese of Santa Fe, 1678–1900* (Washington, 1957); David J. Weber, "The New Mexico Archives in 1827," *NMHR* 61 (January 1986): 53–61; Olmstead, *New Mexico Censuses;* Henry P. Beers, *Spanish and Mexican Records of the American Southwest* (Tucson: University of Arizona Press, 1979); Gerald Thompson, "New Mexico History in *New Mexico Magazine:* An Annotated Bibliography," *Arizona and the West* 17 (Autumn and Winter 1975): 245–78, 339–74; Richard Salazar, *Spanish Archives of New Mexico* (Santa Fe: New Mexico Records Center and Archives); Daniel Tyler, *Sources for New Mexico History, 1821–1848* (Santa Fe: Museum of New Mexico Press, 1984). When one compares Alicia V. Tjarks, "Demographic, Ethnic, and Occupational Structure of New Mexico, 1790: The Census Report of 1790," *The Americas* 35 (July 1978): 45–88, with Antonio José Rios-Bustamante, "New Mexico in the Eighteenth Century: Life, Labor, and Trade in La Villa de San Felipe de Albuquerque, 1706–1790," *Aztlan* 7 (Fall 1976): 357–90, one is astonished at the different conclusions based on the same basic information.

29
Richard Salazar's calendar points the way to additional discoveries, e.g., SANM, II, roll 6, Juan Bautista Vigil to *Gefe Político* Bartolome Baca on business and political affairs. Several other items will prove to be of help, including roll 6, frame 1227, an 1836 list of Santa Fe property owners by street. Tyler, *Sources*, lists several items that should add considerably to an understanding of New Mexican merchants—e.g., Manuel Alvarez Papers; Felipe Chávez Papers (see Gilberto Espinosa and Tibo Chávez, *Rio Abajo* [Pampa,

Texas: n.d.] for one of the better accounts of Felipe Chávez as well as the Belen and Los Chávez settlements); Felipe Delgado Papers, 1704–1912; Extranjero/Anglo Traders Collection, 1823–1848; Marquez y Melo Papers, 1819–1824 (Prominent Chihuahua–Santa Fe trader); Perea Family Papers, 1697–1897 (Romero, García, Chávez, and Perea); José Felipe Chávez Papers, 1739–1936; New Mexico Passport Records, X, Y, 1835–1853 (immigration from other states).

30
Francisco De Thoma, *Historia Popular de Nuevo México, desde su descubrimiento hasta la actualidad* (New York: American Book Company, 1896).

31
The reported advice given by New Mexican merchant Don Mariano José Chávez to his son, "The heretics are going to over-run all this country. Go and learn their language and come back prepared to defend your people," before he was sent to a school in St. Louis in 1841 seems to be an example of the presentism of the territorial period writers. Perhaps the romantic tale is true, but more likely the story served the territorial era politics of Colonel José Francisco Chávez (David J. Weber, *Mexican Frontier*, 234). Weber's source is Howard Lamar, *The Far Southwest, 1846–1912* (New York: Norton, 1970), 49. But Lamar's citation is Marion Dargan, "New Mexico's Fight for Statehood, 1895–1912," *NMHR* 14 (January, April 1939): 181. However, Dargan's articles do not contain this tale and it is not on this page. The quotation is included in Paul A. F. Walter's portion of the *Biography of Colonel José Francisco Chávez, 1833–1924* [1904] (Santa Fe: Historical Society of New Mexico, 1926). But Walter would have this eight-year-old child attending St. Louis University, and the Frank W. Clancy portion discounts that story. Perhaps Walter confused Miguel A. Otero I with Chávez. Otero's son, the territorial governor, reports that his father attended St. Louis University in 1841 and was recalled in 1846. Gilberto Espinosa, "Family Chronicle," *New Mexico Magazine* 45 (February 1967): 28–29, 36, repeats the story, but Espinosa has José Francisco Chávez going with his cousins Joaquín and Francisco Perea to Independence and then to St. Louis in 1843. Espinosa also has the parents Juan Perea and [Mariano] José Chávez accompanying them and reports that José Francisco Chávez went as a child to New York. As most sources have him returning after completing a stint in law and in medicine before he is twenty years old, one has to believe that someone embellished a few stories. Francisco Perea reported that he, his brother, and their young cousin went to school in 1838 in Santa Fe.

32
H. Bailey Carroll and J. Villasana Haggard, trans. and eds., *Three New Mexico Chronicles: The Exposición of Don Pedro Bautista Pino, 1812; the Ojeada of Lic. Antonio Barreiro, 1832; and the Additions by Don Jose Agustin de Escudero, 1849* (Albuquerque: The Quivira Society, 1942).

33
Rodolfo Acuña, *Occupied America: A History of Chicanos*, 2d ed. (New York: Harper & Row, 1981); Tomas Almaguer, "Interpreting Chicano History: The World-System Approach to Nineteenth-Century California," *Review* 4 (Winter 1981): 459–508; Rios-Bustamante, "Albuquerque, 1706–1790"; Ramon A. Gutiérrez, "Honor Ideology, Marriage Negotiation, and Class-Gender Domination in New Mexico, 1690–1846," *Latin American Perspectives* 12 (Winter 1985): 81–104.

34
Acuña, *Occupied America*, 48.

35
While all historians are not as quick to condemn as Acuña, a continued pattern of misunderstanding remains among historical works that touch on the New Mexican merchants. Bruce Johansen and Roberto Maestas in *El Pueblo* appear blessed with secret information unavailable to anyone else, making assertions that cannot be substantiated. An example of this occurs when they discuss the Spanish census of 1776 and say "many were Jewish, although they rarely declared this fact to the government." Their cursory treatment of the Mexican period relies on their well of secret information (Bruce Johansen and Roberto Maestas, *El Pueblo: The Gallegos Family's American Journey, 1503–1980* [New York: Monthly Review Press, 1983]).

36
Paul Horgan, *Great River* (New York: Minerva Press, 1968); Lamar, *Far Southwest;* Weber, *Mexican Frontier,* 125–130. These three works do not pretend to deal comprehensively with the Santa Fe Trail but do draw some conclusions based on historians' treatment of the trade. That they mention New Mexicans as merchants is commendable. Leo E. Oliva, *Soldiers on the Santa Fe Trail* (Norman: University of Oklahoma Press, 1967), offers a glimpse of potential wealth, especially when he treats the caravans of 1846. He asserts that the New Mexican "upper, ruling classes were hostile" (p. 70) and prepared for war. Oliva also makes reference to the belief that Manuel Armijo was involved in shipping a "large quantity" of weapons and labels these items "contraband" (p. 64). The secretary of the treasury approved the legal shipment of products, and the Harmony claim for damages should cast a new light on that caravan as well as the role of New Mexican merchants.

37
W. H. Timmons, "The El Paso Area in the Mexican Period, 1821–1848," *Southwestern Historical Quarterly* 84 (July 1980): 1–28, provides genealogical material for James Magoffin and includes the perspective of American merchants in El Paso concerning the war; he differentiates between pre- and post-1840 merchants. John O. Baxter, "Salvador Armijo: Citizen of Albuquerque, 1823–1879," *NMHR* 53 (July 1978): 219–37, details familial relationships and touches upon occupations. Ruth Armstrong, "San Miguel: Port of Entry on the Santa Fe Trail," *New Mexico Magazine* 46 (February 1968): 10–13, describes a community but the nature of the system is little revealed. Marc Simmons, *The Little Lion of the Southwest: A Life of Manuel Antonio Chaves* (Chicago: Sage Books, 1973), a biography not dealing directly with a New Mexican merchant, serves as a rare example of careful craftsmanship and demonstrates the potential wealth of the era, the people, and the Santa Fe Trail. Daniel Tyler, "Anglo-American Penetration of the Southwest: The View from New Mexico," *Southwestern Historical Quarterly* 75 (January 1972): 325, deals with the Anglo view from New Mexico. See also Daniel Tyler, "Gringo Views of Governor Manuel Armijo," *NMHR* 45 (January 1970): 23–46. Janet Lecompte, in "Manuel Armijo's Family History," *NMHR* 48 (July 1973): 251–58, helps define just who the Armijos were and will help ferret out just who was actually concerned. Ward Alan Minge, "The Last Will and Testament of Don Severino Martínez," *New Mexico Quarterly* 33 (Spring 1963): 33–56, demonstrates the impact of the trail on material culture. See also Lynn Perrigo,

"New Mexico in the Mexican Period as Revealed in the Torres Documents," *NMHR* 29 (January 1954): 28–40; David J. Weber, *Arms, Indians, and the Mismanagement of New Mexico* (El Paso: University of Texas at El Paso, Southwestern Studies Series No. 77, 1986); Richard Nostrand, "Mexican Americans Circa 1850," *Annals of the Association of American Geographers* 65 (September 1975): 378–90; Oakah L. Jones, *Los Paisanos: Spanish Settlers on the Northern Frontier of New Spain* (Norman: University of Oklahoma Press, 1979); and Frances L. Swadesh, *Los Primeros Pobladores: Hispanic Americans of the Ute Frontier* (Notre Dame: University of Notre Dame Press, 1974).

ESSAY EIGHT

David Dary

Storied Silver, Fabled Gold
Buried Treasure Legends along the Santa Fe Trail

About the author
David Dary is a professor of journalism and director of the H. H. Herbert School of Journalism and Mass Communication at the University of Oklahoma in Norman. He is the author of *The Buffalo Book* (1974, revised 1988), *True Tales of the Old-Time Plains* (1978), *Cowboy Culture* (1981), *True Tales of Old-Time Kansas* (1984), *Entrepreneurs of the Old West* (1986), *Kanzana 1854–1900: A Selected Bibliography of Books, Pamphlets and Ephemera of Kansas* (1986), and *More True Tales of Old-Time Kansas* (1987). A winner of the Wrangler Award from the National Cowboy Hall of Fame, a Spur Award, and the Westerners' Best Nonfiction Book of 1981 Award, he is a former president of the Western Writers of America and Westerners International and is currently chairman of the board of the Westerners International Foundation and a member of the board of directors of the Oklahoma Historical Society.

Essays and Monographs

POSSIBLY the wildest of wild goose chases in the recorded history of what is today the United States was Coronado's search for the fabled Quivira, or Seven Cities of Cibola. The treasure-seeking Spaniards wandered over more than 3,000 miles of land previously unexplored by Europeans, much of it plains, in search of the cities where streets supposedly were paved with gold.

Today there are many legends of lost mines and buried treasure along the route believed taken by Coronado and the other Spanish explorers who followed. Countless other treasure legends exist along many other trails used by explorers, gold miners, outlaws, settlers, wagon freighters, and traders who crisscrossed the Great Plains and eastern slopes of the Rocky Mountains. At least one traditional buried treasure legend is undoubtedly associated with each county of each state between Texas and Canada and from Missouri to the Rockies—and this is a conservative estimate.

Some of the more interesting buried treasure legends are linked in one manner or another with the Santa Fe Trail. Most of these have some basis in fact, and in a few instances there is good reason to think that the treasures may exist, but many amount to no more than wishful thinking on the part of those who have passed them down from generation to generation.

THE MILT BRYAN TREASURE TALE[1]

Perhaps the earliest legend of buried treasure along the Santa Fe Trail is dated 1828, seven years after William Becknell and his party reached Santa Fe and thereby opened trade between Missouri and New Mexico. On the first day of September 1828, a party of twenty Missourians, including a young man named Milt Bryan, rode slowly out of Santa Fe after completing several weeks of successful trading.

The caravan consisted of four horse-drawn wagons carrying supplies and several thousand dollars in Mexican silver coin. Behind the wagons a few men herded 150 mules and horses that the party hoped to sell in Missouri. The captain of the caravan was a seasoned plainsman named John Means.

For the first few days their journey was uneventful. But after they crossed the Cimarron River in what is today the Oklahoma Panhandle, the traders occasionally saw Indians watching them from a distance. One afternoon, as they crossed a rise, they suddenly found themselves entering a large camp of Comanches.

Storied Silver, Fabled Gold

As Bryan later recalled, the traders could neither turn back nor move to either side to avoid the Comanche camp.

With guns drawn, they slowly continued along the trail. Soon a Comanche chief greeted them and told them they must stay the night. He said his young men would guard their stock and that his people had plenty of buffalo meat to feed them. Captain Means turned down the chief's invitation and gave the signal for the caravan to hurry along. As Bryan later wrote, Captain Means, Thomas Ellison, and himself—all on horseback—were a little behind the wagons, horses, and mules. Suddenly, he said, some of the Indians seized the traders' bridle reins while others began firing arrows at the caravan. Ellison and Bryan spurred their horses and broke the Indians' hold, but Means was hit and fell, mortally wounded, to the ground.

As Bryan recalled, he and Ellison chased after the caravan, which was racing away from the camp. Many of the Indians jumped on their ponies and rode in pursuit. The traders kept on going, managing somehow to fight off the Indians until the wagons were about a half mile away. There they circled the four wagons and established their own camp, still firing at the Indians, who kept their distance.

The traders were kept busy all night fighting off handfuls of Comanches who tried to sneak into the wagon circle. At the first light of dawn, the trading party moved out on the trail, only to be attacked again. That day they made only five miles—not the fifteen or more that they normally averaged on the trail.

During the next four days the Indians continued the harassment. They would surround the train, attack it, and ride off. They kept this pattern up, apparently recognizing that the traders were becoming exhausted from fatigue and loss of sleep. On the morning of the sixth day, as the Means party moved onto the broad plains, they found no Indians, but around noon they were attacked again. This was the largest group of Comanches the traders had yet seen, and before Bryan and the others knew what was happening, they had stampeded some 150 loose horses and mules.

The men quickly corralled their wagons and built a breastwork of harnesses and saddles. Barely had they finished this fortification, however, than the Indians charged again. The attackers returned several times before nightfall, and each time the traders fought them off. Later that night, when the moon went down about two hours after dark, there was a strange quiet on the plains. As Bryan later told the story, the traders talked among themselves about what to do next. While they did have a good supply of ammunition, they realized that they were 500 miles from Missouri. In a desperate gamble, they decided to leave their wagons and escape on foot under cover of darkness.

Each man filled his pockets with silver coins, but together they could not carry all of their trading profits. Bryan recalled that they left a large amount of silver but did not say whether it was buried or left in the wagons. According to his description, the spot where they abandoned their camp and the remaining silver is approximately twenty to thirty miles northeast of Upper Springs on the Santa Fe Trail along the present border of northern Oklahoma and southeastern Colorado.

The traders slipped away from the wagons and began walking north, away from the trail, in the hope that the Indians would assume that they had continued traveling east. Eventually the party reached the Arkansas River in present Kearny County, Kansas, and then turned toward their destination, traversing all of Kansas on foot until they arrived safely in Missouri.

The following year Bryan again traveled the Santa Fe Trail, but there is no record that he or any of his partners recovered the silver they had left near Upper Springs in the fall of 1828.

THE TREASURE OF DON ANTONIO JOSÉ CHÁVEZ[2]

In february of 1843 a Santa Fe Trail trader named Don Antonio José Chávez set out from Santa Fe for Missouri with two wagons and five men. The winter had been mild; otherwise, they probably would have waited another month to begin their journey east. Their wagons were loaded with furs that Chávez had obtained in trade with mountain men and perhaps Indians in and around Santa Fe. Chávez planned to sell the furs for a nice profit in Missouri. In one of his wagons he also carried $25,000 in specie and gold, presumably to buy merchandise in the States, take it back to Santa Fe, and sell it for a profit.

When Chávez left Santa Fe he also had fifty-five head of mules, many of which he used to pull his two heavily laden wagons. The journey along the trail was uneventful until the small caravan pushed east past the great bend of the Arkansas River. Then, as a winter storm swept out of the Rockies, the weather became bitterly cold. At a spot about four miles southeast of present-day Lyons, Kansas, just north of today's Saxmon, Chávez and his party were forced to make a temporary winter camp on the banks of Jarvis Creek. Within a day or two fifty of Chávez's mules had died from exposure, and when the weather warmed it was impossible for the party, with but five weak mules left, to pull even one of the wagons. They were stranded and had no choice but to wait until another wagon train happened along. For security, Chávez buried his treasure near the little creek.

Early one afternoon a few days later, fifteen men rode into Chávez's camp. They were led by John McDaniel, who claimed to hold a commission as a captain in the Texas army. At the time, the Republic of Texas claimed a large slice of what is now southwest Kansas south of the Arkansas River, and it was having increased difficulty with Mexico. McDaniel and his men, who actually were nothing more than outlaws, reputedly were heading west to join Texas forces which had been ordered by the president of the Republic, Sam Houston, to capture property carried by Mexican traders passing through Texas territory.

When McDaniel saw that the men of the Chávez party were Mexicans, he and his group immediately took them prisoner and robbed them of their belongings, dividing the booty among themselves. Seven of McDaniel's men then announced that they were returning to Missouri, and when morning came they loaded their spoils on Chávez's five mules and rode away. McDaniel and his remaining companions, however, stayed in camp in the belief that more plunder was to be had. McDaniel searched Chávez again, found a small sum of money hidden in the trader's clothing, and demanded to know if there was any more. Chávez refused to answer. When McDaniel beat him, the old trader remained silent. After another round of beating, Chávez admitted that there was more money but refused to say where it was buried.

For two days the stalemate continued. As a last resort, the Missourian lined up Chávez's five men and, in an effort to force him to talk, had them shot down one by one in cold blood. Chávez still kept his silence. Then, having lost all patience, McDaniel led the trader to a nearby ravine that emptied into the creek and posed the question one last time. When Chávez, defiant to the end, still refused to answer, McDaniel shot and killed him. In the aftermath of the carnage, the murderers loaded the bodies of the six traders

Essays and Monographs

onto one of the wagons, pushed it into the creek, and rode away with whatever goods were at hand.

Whether one of McDaniel's men bragged about the attack or one of Chávez's men survived it is not clear. Nevertheless, an expedition of U.S. troops sent out by Colonel Stephen Watts Kearny caught McDaniel and several of his party. They were tried in St. Louis for the crimes. And it was while McDaniel was on the witness stand that he disclosed the existence of the Chávez treasure and gave birth to the legend.

Following the establishment of Kansas Territory in 1854 and the state of Kansas in 1861, people familiar with the story searched for the Chávez treasure. One account relates how a party of men, strangers to what is now Rice County, camped on Jarvis Creek during the late 1860s. An early resident, M. F. Baker, recalled that the men camped on the spot where Chávez and his party had been killed. After the strangers left the area, residents found that the straw floor of their tent site covered a deep pit at the bottom of which, some of them claimed, was the imprint of a large iron kettle. Others, however, said that the pit revealed nothing but shadows.

THE HARVEYVILLE TREASURE LEGEND[3]

Occasionally, while researching a buried treasure legend, one encounters a tale that does not ring true. Something about it insists that the events related in the tale are highly unlikely. Sometimes careful research confirms the suspicion. Such is the case of a buried treasure legend set along the Santa Fe Trail in southeast Wabaunsee County, Kansas, long before Kansas Territory was established.

This tale first surfaced in Matt Thomson's 1901 book *The Early History of Wabaunsee County*. Thomson's story goes something like this: During 1842 and 1843, several wagon trains were robbed by a gang of outlaws as they followed the Santa Fe Trail between 110 Mile Creek in modern Osage County and Big John Springs just east of Council Grove. Soldiers supposedly were sent out from Fort Leavenworth to search for the outlaws but without success. Freighters were warned to be on their guard against the outlaws.

As Thompson tells the story, a mule-drawn train of forty-three wagons made camp late on a spring afternoon in 1844 about 200 yards west of Log Chain Creek near the present Wabaunsee County line. The wagon train was owned by an American but manned by Mexican teamsters. It was attacked by a gang of twenty-one

Storied Silver, Fabled Gold

outlaws, who killed twenty-seven of the forty-three teamsters in the train. The American owner managed to evade the outlaws and escape.

While some of the outlaws held the teamsters prisoner, others rummaged through the wagons and found an iron box 18 x 12 x 8 inches which held, according to the story, $75,000 in gold. The outlaws took the box and made off with about 500 mules that had been used to pull the train's wagons.

The story is a bit vague at this point, but apparently the owner of the wagon train later returned to the camp, told one teamster to take charge, and then got a horse and rode to Fort Leavenworth for help. A company of cavalry accompanied him to the scene of the raid, arriving four days after the event.

After burying the dead teamsters, the soldiers tried to follow the outlaws' trail, but the herd of mules had been split and driven in two different directions. Following one of the trails that led west, the company arrived a few days later at the Little Arkansas River about midway between present Lyons and McPherson, Kansas. There they met an old trapper, H. B. Hobbs. When the officer in charge told Hobbs the story, the plainsman agreed to act as a guide. He knew the country, he said, and he soon concluded that the outlaws would not dare take the mules to Missouri or to New Mexico. The only safe market, he stated, was Oregon.

With this in mind, as the story goes, Hobbs led the soldiers in a northwesterly direction. A few days later they came upon the fresh trail of the outlaws and the stolen mules. It appeared that the split herd had been brought together. The trail headed west along the Smoky Hill River. The soldiers followed and somewhere in present Logan County, near Russell Springs, Kansas, they came upon the outlaws and the stolen animals. A battle ensued in which fourteen of the outlaws were killed. The surviving five outlaws were taken to Fort Leavenworth, where they were tried and sentenced to life imprisonment in federal prison at Alton, Illinois. The mules were returned to the owner of the wagon train, but the iron box reportedly containing $75,000 in gold was not recovered.

Matt Thomson's 1901 story, however, does not stop there. He relates how the military concluded that two missing outlaws—twenty-one had attacked the wagon train and only nineteen were accounted for—had not traveled with the others. And the two missing outlaws were thought to have had the still-missing gold.

Essays and Monographs

The events of the story, Thomson states, were forgotten until 1857, when a man named Allen Hodgson settled in the vicinity of the mound that supposedly had been used as a lookout by the outlaws years before. Hodgson claimed that he had found the ashes and an outline of a log cabin, and Hodgson's son Ira, apparently Thomson's primary source for the story, recalled how an old plainsman named Tom Fulton had related the story of the outlaws and the robbery.

Thomson tells how Ira Hodgson recalled that there was much talk among employees of the Overland Mail Company about a treasure being buried somewhere between 110 Mile Creek and Big John Springs along the Santa Fe Trail. Some employees, Hodgson claimed, had searched for it but had found nothing. Then Hodgson told how in 1867 a man claiming to have come from Alton, Illinois, where five of the outlaws had been jailed for life, spent the summer months unsuccessfully searching for the treasure along Big John Springs, Rock, Bluff, and 142 Mile creeks.

Jumping ahead a few years, Thomson then relates how in the summer of 1895 an Englishman who was a preacher arrived in Harveyville. Aside from occasional sermons, he did a great deal of fishing. His favorite fishing spot was near the mouth of Bachelor's branch close by the cabin of the outlaws. Some people wondered why the preacher spent his time fishing there since it was one of the poorest fishing holes in the county. Then, one September day, according to Thomson, the preacher disappeared. Within a few days someone discovered a hole in the ground north of the Harveyville cemetery on the site of the old outlaw cabin. The hole was about four feet deep, and on its sides people claimed to have seen the imprint of an iron box 18 x 12 x 8 inches. Iron rust supposedly was still visible, sticking to the earth. The witnesses concluded that the preacher had found the iron box containing the gold which had been taken from the wagon train raid fifty-one years earlier.

That's the story as told by Matt Thomson in 1901.

But efforts to confirm the facts were unsuccessful. No record of an 1842 wagon train raid could be found in Missouri newspapers, and such raids were reported. And no military records exist confirming the army's involvement or its battle with the outlaws in what is now Logan County. On the contrary, tucked away in the manuscript section of the Kansas State Historical Society in Topeka are two letters relating to the tale, and they confirm that it is a hoax.

One letter, dated February 10, 1903, was written by S. B. Harvey, who had settled in the area in August of 1854 and for whom Harveyville, Kansas, is named; the other was written by Stephen J. Spear later in 1903. Harvey wrote that he "never saw a vestige of a former "Robbers' Roost" near Harveyville, and he noted, "I do not think such a place ever existed in the neighborhood." Spear, in his letter, fully explained how the hoax was created. "In the fall of 1891," he states,

> William Wetzel, Jr., made a fishing trip on Dragoon Creek, near its confluence with Bachelor Creek. On his return trip . . . he discovered what he thought was an Indian grave. Some days later he took a spade and went unobserved to this place, hoping by digging to uncover some Indian relics. He dug a hole about six feet long north and south, and two feet wide, and about three feet deep in the center. Not finding any signs of Indian relics he then dug another hole about 18 inches long, 12 inches wide and 8 inches deep in the bottom of the larger excavation, but discovered nothing. He returned home without having refilled the hole. A short time after this he happened to be in Harveyville one evening and proposed to some boys to go coon hunting. The plan met with approval and a short time later a gang of about eight or ten boys, William Wetzel at the head and armed with a lantern, were on their way. . . . After leading the boys around through the woods for awhile, William at length brought them up at the scene of his recent digging. Feigning surprise at finding such a hole he exclaimed: "I wonder what this is?" The story of the hole soon went the rounds of the community, and during the next few days there were several investigations to find if some treasure had been taken away. William Wetzel some time later gave the writer the particulars of the above.

Spear recalled that not long after Wetzel had perpetrated his joke, Ira Hodgson recalled the story he had heard from the old plainsman, Tom Fulton. It was then that people in Harveyville began to discuss the tale of the buried treasure, including the story of the old English preacher—who, Spear states in his account, had not disappeared at all but had gone to Burlingame, Kansas, to preach.

The testimony of Spear and Harvey, in addition to the total lack of evidence supporting the tale, leave little doubt that the legend of buried treasure along the Santa Fe Trail near Harveyville has no basis in fact.

THE LIGHTNER RANCH TREASURE LEGEND[4]

In 1851 a small wagon train of 49ers was returning east from the California gold fields. According to tradition, members of the party had struck it rich. On their return, traveling the southern route across what is now Arizona and New Mexico to Santa Fe, they met the Santa Fe Trail and headed toward Missouri. Their journey was apparently uneventful until they reached the Arkansas River a few miles south of modern Offerle, Kansas. There they camped for the night on the south side of the river on land that later became part of the Lightner Ranch.

Early the following morning, as the travelers were breaking camp, someone in the group saw a party of Indians approaching in the distance. Fearing the worst, the 49ers quickly forded the river and, once on the other side, prepared to do battle. Meanwhile, two of the men buried their gold in a Dutch oven under a small tree. Then, according to the story, the worst *did* happen: the Indians, who outnumbered the 49ers, charged across the river and killed all of them except one. The lone survivor supposedly was an eight-year-old girl, who was taken captive.

What happened to the little girl is not known, but later events suggest that she may have survived. About 1918 a woman arrived in Kinsley, the county seat of Edwards County, and hired a local driver, Lee Smith, to take her in his Maxwell to a place on the Arkansas River south of town. On the drive, Smith said, the woman kept looking at maps and checking a notebook. The woman appeared to know exactly where she wanted to go, and they ended up at the old Santa Fe Trail crossing. Once there, she convinced Smith to drive to the other side, and he forded the river in his Maxwell.

Here the woman located several mounds of earth about seventy-five feet beyond the crossing. Pointing to the mounds, she told Smith that she believed that people from a wagon train, killed by Indians years before, were buried there. Still very much in the dark, Smith began to question her. She told him only that she lived in the

East and was a relative of someone who had escaped the massacre. Although she spent some time looking over the ground and poked around a large old tree, Smith stated that she found nothing. Later he drove her back to Kinsley, and he never saw her again.

The woman apparently did not return to Edwards County, and no one has ever admitted finding a buried treasure at the crossing. Old-timers in the county recalled years ago that a boy once found a gold wedding band buried in the sand near the crossing, but there is no proof that it was connected with anyone in the party of 49ers. The strongest evidence that a wagon train was actually destroyed there was turned up years ago by Wilbur Oliphant, who once lived and worked at the old Lightner Ranch. Once, as he was digging a hole near the crossing to bury a dead horse, he found the remains of old wagons whose iron parts included wheels, rims, and frames that were still in fairly good condition. It seems likely that they could have been the remains of the destroyed wagon train, but Oliphant found no Dutch oven filled with gold.

THE TREASURE LEGEND OF JESUS M. MARTINEZ[5]

Late on a summer day in 1853, Jesus M. Martinez's wagon train came to a halt on the sun-scorched plains just west of modern Dodge City, Kansas. Shortly before sunset, Martinez ordered his men to draw their wagons into a tight circle and to prepare camp for the night. Following their evening meal, the men began to relax. It had been a hot day.

Martinez, an old hand at taking wagon trains back and forth between Santa Fe and Missouri, posted his usual guards against the three evils of trail travel—Indians, bandits, and prairie fires. Although Indians had been spotted during the day at some distance, they did not appear to be hostile, and Martinez's wagon train, consisting of eighty-two men and 120 wagons, was large. Some of the wagons were hooked in tandem, and each man was armed. Before going to sleep, however, Martinez checked his wagons. He made sure that one of them, which carried thousands of dollars in Mexican silver, was secure. Then he went to bed.

During the night the camp was peaceful, but early in the morning, as the moon climbed high in the night sky, some of the teamsters' dogs started barking. At the same time, the guards saw what appeared to be moving shadows not far from camp, and they immediately woke their captain. Understanding Indian tactics,

Martinez ordered all of his men to prepare for an attack at dawn. The teamsters quickly dug trenches, built dirt mounds, checked their guns and powder, and waited for the attack.

At the first faint light of dawn, it came. Yelling and shouting, the Indians charged the camp from all sides, but Martinez and his men where ready. They fired their weapons, felling some of the Indians and wounding others. The attacking party withdrew to regroup, and the teamsters waited for the anticipated second charge, which came an hour later.

Throughout the morning and into the early afternoon the Indians charged at regular intervals, but each time the teamsters fought them off. The siege continued into the second night, then a second day and a third night. For five days the battle raged. Only a handful of Martinez's men were killed or wounded, while the Indian toll was high. By the sixth night, however, the tired teamsters were running low on ammunition. They had hoped that the Indians—apparently Cheyennes, Arapahos, and Kiowas— would soon give up and leave. Instead, the Indians made a massive, desperate attack on the circled wagons, and in resisting the onslaught the teamsters used up all their powder. Before long, the Indians had overrun the wagon train.

Supposedly, every man was killed except Martinez, who, under cover of darkness, hid from the Indians as they looted the wagons, robbed the dead teamsters, and set fire to the camp. Martinez stayed put until the first rays of morning light broke on the horizon. Then he crept from his hiding place and, seeing that he was alone, searched through the charred wagons. To his surprise, much of the silver remained—twenty-one small bags, each containing a thousand Mexican dollars. Martinez buried these in the ground near the burned-out camp.

During the weeks that followed, Martinez made his way back to Mexico, where his health failed. According to tradition, on his deathbed he told his son about the silver and described the spot where he had buried it. For several years after his father's death, the young Martinez gave little thought to the treasure, but as he grew older he decided to search for it. Making his way to Kansas in the early 1870s, he discovered that Fort Dodge and the town of Dodge City had grown up near the site of the massacre. Along with another man to whom he revealed the secret of the buried silver, he located the remains of the wagon train. Using a sharpened wire, he spent several days probing the plains around the site, but to no avail. When his patience wore out, he returned to Mexico, but the pits and dirt piles of his effort were still plainly visible in the area into the early twentieth century.

THE MORTON COUNTY TREASURE LEGENDS[6]

Located in the southwestern corner of Kansas, Morton County borders on Colorado to the west and on Oklahoma to the south. The Cimarron Cutoff or "dry route" of the Santa Fe Trail once traversed the southwestern portion of the county. Here, along the Cimarron River, lay Point of Rocks Ranch, which took its name from high sandstone bluffs along the river. Travelers following the Santa Fe Trail called the bluff Point Rocks, and the Spanish referred to them as Mesa Blanco. Two treasure legends are linked to this region of the trail.

The first tale involves a party of 49ers returning east from the California gold fields about 1851. According to the legend, robbers took more than $90,000 in gold from the party. Before they could escape with the loot, however, they saw another party of travelers approaching. Since the gold was quite heavy and the bandits could not flee quickly, they reportedly buried it in the vicinity of Point of Rocks and for some reason never returned to dig it up.

The second tale involves a man named Alexander and four other men who during the early 1850s left their homes in Illinois with three wagons loaded with dry goods. Tradition has it that they traveled safely to Santa Fe, where they sold their goods, mostly calico, for two dollars a yard, and received payment in silverware, silver bars, and silver bullion. Then they started back along the trail.

Near Point of Rocks the traders made camp, only to be surprised during the night by Indians who drove off their livestock. Exactly what happened next is unclear, but the men, apparently fearing that the Indians would return at dawn, buried their silver in the ground, pushed their wagons over the spot where the treasure lay buried, and set the wagons afire. Fleeing their camp, they watched the wagons burn from a distance until only a few coals could be seen at dawn. They then began walking east toward Missouri. Apparently they returned to their homes in Illinois, and there is no evidence that they ever recovered their buried silver on the Cimarron River.

Most historians have ignored buried treasure legends, perhaps believing that they belong to the discipline of the folklorist. Yet because many such legends contain some basis of historical fact, they are justifiably part of history and should be treated as such. J. Fairfax-Blakesborough perhaps best expressed their value many years ago when he wrote:

> When a land forgets its legends,
> Sees but falsehoods in its past,
> When a nation views its sires
> In the light of fools and liars—
> 'Tis a sign of its decline
> And its glories cannot last.

Storied Silver, Fabled Gold

1
Milton E. Bryan's treasure legend is based on Bryan's reminiscences. I used the original manuscript of Bryan's 1828 journey given to me by his great-great-great-grandson, James Stuppy, after he read a shorter version of Bryan's story that I put on paper for *Star* magazine, the *Kansas City Star*, February 8, 1976. Bryan's account was first published under the title "The Flight of Time" in *The Kansas Chief*, Troy, Kansas, June 9, 1887. An undated clipping from a Seneca, Kansas, newspaper (not identified) provided by Mr. Stuppy mentioned that the reminiscences were presented as a speech by Bryan in May 1885, at Wathena, Kansas. The late Henry Inman published an abbreviated version of Bryan's adventures in his book *The Old Santa Fé Trail* (New York: Macmillan, 1897), but Inman insisted on calling Bryan "Mr. Bryant." A longer version detailing all of Bryan's adventures in 1828 and 1829 plus his later life may be found in David Dary, *True Tales of Old-Time Kansas* (Lawrence: University Press of Kansas, 1984), 2–11.

2
Perhaps the earliest publication of this legend, aside from newspaper stories, was in A. T. Andreas's *History of the State of Kansas* (Chicago: A. T. Andreas, 1883), 56. It is repeated in William Connelley's *A Standard History of Kansas and Kansans*, Vol 1 (New York: Lewis Co., 1918), 120. A review of the legend plus an account of one search for the treasure appears in the *Wichita* (Kansas) *Eagle*, May 15, 1931.

3
As related in the above, the treasure tale appears in Matt Thomson's *The Early History of Wabaunsee County, Kansas . . .* published in Alma, Kansas, in 1901. The chapter containing the tale is entitled "The First Log House" and appears on pages 141–45. Samuel B. Harvey's letter was written on February 10, 1903, to Stephen Jackson Spear. Spear's subsequent account was written later in 1903. Both documents are in the manuscript section of the Kansas State Historical Society, Topeka. Additional background on the early settlement of the area may be found in Spear's "Reminiscences of the Early Settlement of Dragoon Creek, Wabaunsee County," appearing in *Kansas Historical Society Collections* 13:345–63. Spear was born in Connecticut in 1838 and died in Burlingame, Kansas, in 1904. He first settled in Wabaunsee County in 1858 and served in the Kansas legislature in 1865 and 1866.

4
I first ran across this tale in a scrapbook containing Edwards County, Kansas, newspaper clippings in the library of the Kansas State Historical Society, Topeka. A January 9, 1936, story headlined "Renew Search for Treasure Buried in Sands near Offerle" told about Wilbur Oliphant's experiences and those of Lee Smith. A later newspaper story, published in the *Kansas City Times*, March 9, 1953, repeated the story, but claimed the treasure was buried in buckskin bags and amounted to $50,000 in gold dust. It is possible the bags were inside the Dutch oven. A search of government records, Santa Fe Trail narratives, and related documents has failed to turn up confirmation of the massacre in what is today Edwards County, Kansas. Even Robert Wright's book *Dodge City, The Cowboy Capital* (Wichita: Eagle Press, 1913) does not include mention of the tale, although several other treasure tales are told. Dodge City is about twenty-five miles southwest of where the massacre supposedly occurred.

5
An early newspaper account of this tale appears as an article entitled "A

Essays and Monographs

Strange Story" in the *Dodge City* (Kansas) *Times,* September 22, 1877. In the article the writer—not identified—observes: "This story, as told above, is a historical fact, and portions of it have been heretofore published. We can give names of men who know more about it than we do, but by request we do not publish them." Robert Wright later quoted the article in *Dodge City, Cowboy Capital,* 17-20.

6
The only source for the tale of the Illinois traders is an article published by the *Kansas City Times,* March 9, 1953. The other tale concerning a robbery is contained in an old undated newspaper clipping in the author's collection.

ESSAY NINE

Jack D. Rittenhouse

The Literature of the Santa Fe Trail

An Introduction and Guide for the New Traveler

About the author
Jack D. Rittenhouse is compiler of *The Santa Fe Trail: A Historical Bibliography* (1971), which won the Award of Merit from the National Association for State and Local History in 1972. He was editor of books on the American West at the University of New Mexico Press, 1968–1978, and since his retirement has been a rare book dealer in Albuquerque. He is a past president of the Historical Society of New Mexico and from 1960 to 1968 was active in his own private Stagecoach Press, which published fifty books on the West.

IN THE PAST FEW YEARS America has become fascinated with its historic trails. The interest was always there, of course, especially in the adventure and romance, but now we want to go beyond armchair entertainment. In the past several years, an association was formed for those interested in the Lewis and Clark Trail. Another was more recently formed for those concerned with the California-Oregon Trail. A foundation has been organized to correlate studies of old Highway 66. Now we are focusing on the Santa Fe Trail.

This new, increasing interest grows out of a generally rising interest in the American West. Americans are great travelers and they want to understand what they are seeing. The center of population is shifting to the West, and new residents want to learn about their new home. Those whose families have lived for generations in the West—so long that no one now living can give a firsthand account—seek their roots in the past.

Of course, it all started with the literature of the trails. In the beginning was the word, and for the Santa Fe Trail the word probably was Pike. It was Pike's account of his travels to the southern Rockies, first published in 1810, that may have given Missourians the idea that there was a nation already existing to the west and southwest. Soon the trappers, then the traders, and then the wagons were moving west.

Today a truly fine collection of the literature about the Santa Fe Trail could encompass perhaps a thousand items. My own published bibliography, issued sixteen years ago, listed some seven hundred items. I will hazard a guess that I missed a hundred nuggets in my search; another hundred items have probably been published since then; and still another hundred lie waiting to be found.

To ask which of the seven hundred books I found to be the most important is like asking what is the most important ingredient in a hunter's stew. The literature must be savored as a whole. But if it is the meat, the substance, you seek, it would be Josiah Gregg's *Commerce of the Prairies*, first published in 1844, five years before Parkman's work on the California-Oregon Trail. From a collector's viewpoint the first edition of Gregg is the one to have; for the student, the most useful is the version annotated by Max Moorhead and published by the University of Oklahoma Press in 1954. The only edition currently in print is the abridged Lakeside Press edition that has been reprinted by the University of Nebraska Press. Without Gregg your collection has no foundation.

If it is flavor you want, read Lewis Garrard's *Wah-to-Yah and the Taos Trail*, Susan Magoffin's *Down the Santa Fe Trail and into Mexico*, or Marian Sloan Russell's memoirs, now available under the title *Land of Enchantment*.

Lewis Garrard was seventeen when he went with a caravan westward along the Santa Fe Trail to Bent's Fort and on to Taos. He was only twenty-one when his book was published in 1850. He described what he saw and where he went—the most useful sort of writing. Lawrence Clark Powell gives the best critique of Garrard in *Southwest Classics:* "Although the result was both history and literature, Garrard was not consciously writing either. He was filtering life through his own sensibilities. We see the Taos world as it was during those wild days of 1847—the sights and smells and the salty lingo to which his ear was so faithful. How he relished it all!" (p. 32). The first reprint of Garrard's book did not appear until 1932; since then there have been reprints by five publishers. Currently a good edition is available in paperback (University of Oklahoma Press) with a fine introduction by A. B. Guthrie, Jr.

Susan Shelby Magoffin was only two years younger than Garrard when she and her husband traveled the Santa Fe Trail in the same year as Garrard—1846. Her diary lay unknown and unpublished until it was discovered by Susan Drumm, librarian of the Missouri Historical Society in St. Louis. With Drumm's annotations, it was published in 1926 by Yale University Press. A reprint in paperback is now available from the University of Nebraska Press.

Marian Sloan Russell was a child of seven when she and her brother first went with their widowed mother, Eliza St. Clair Sloan, over the Santa Fe Trail. They were in a wagon train led by Francois X. Aubry, who was an admirer of Mrs. Sloan. Married in 1865 to a young lieutenant, Marian Russell later made more trips over the trail. Her memoirs ran serially in *The Colorado Magazine* from 1943 to 1944; they were then published in book form by the Branding Iron Press in 1954; and they now appear in paperback (University of New Mexico Press, 1986).

If it is freshness you seek, get Marc Simmons's *Following the Santa Fe Trail*. For general history, start with the works by Colonel Henry Inman, Robert L. Duffus, Margaret Long, and Stanley Vestal. And do not miss David Lavender's *Bent's Fort* or the books by Morris Taylor and by Leo Oliva.

In physical form, the literature about the Santa Fe Trail consists of government reports, maps, books, pamphlets, articles in journals or magazines (often reprinted separately as pamphlets), newspaper articles, broadsides, bits of ephemera such as franked envelopes and posters and stage schedules, photographs, and—of course—unpublished manuscripts. The primary, or firsthand, information consists of diaries, journals, and letters, all written during or soon after the event, and recollections, which may have been written five to fifty years later and thus are subject to the weaknesses of memory. The secondary works—which need not be secondary in importance—are those pieces written, or rather rewritten, by authors who collected and analyzed data.

Except for government reports and Josiah Gregg's *Commerce of the Prairies*, most of the early literature about the trail presented it as an adventure, heading out toward Santa Fe as a golden market. There was much detail on the scenery, on hardships, and on dangers. It was the best of all stories. Henry Inman wrote one of the greatest of these books, *The Old Santa Fé Trail*, first issued in 1897. It was so successful that he wrote a companion book, *Tales of the Trail*, in 1898.

But trails change, not in location so much as in their effect on the economy, commerce, settlement, and the people who travel along them. The Lewis and Clark Trail represents one of exploration into an unknown land; few people, if any, followed that trail later. The Oregon-California Trail was originally a one-way road for emigrants heading west, but it later became a two-way trail. In contrast, the Santa Fe Trail was a two-way trail from the beginning. Most of those who went to Santa Fe probably returned. Until 1845, after crossing the Arkansas its travelers were in either Mexico or in the Republic of Texas. After the end of the Mexican War in 1848, they were on U.S. soil all the way. Thus the literature about the Santa Fe Trail differs from the literature on all other trails.

And the Santa Fe Trail did change. The routes remained fairly stable, for the old wagonmasters knew the best and shortest routes, down to the nearest quarter mile. But settlements sprang up, at first as favored resting spots near landmarks, then as forts or places where one could get repairs, then as small towns. Cultivated lands spread westward. Traffic became heavy and well organized. The land itself was changing. These aspects of the Santa Fe Trail have not been dealt with in the literature and remain to be pursued.

More scholarly attention must also be paid to relations between travelers and Indians along the trail, and little has been done on the west-to-east wagon trains organized by New Mexicans of Spanish descent.

There have been good beginnings for further research in these later books, which changed in viewpoint from the adventurous memoirs of earlier days. For example, Leo E. Oliva's *Soldiers on the Santa Fe Trail* (University of Oklahoma Press, 1967) assesses military activities along the trail, and Seymour V. Connor's and Jimmy M. Skaggs's *Broadcloth and Britches: The Santa Fe Trade* (Texas A&M University Press, 1977) deals with the goods and practices of Santa Fe traders. In the same vein, the late Morris F. Taylor's *First Mail West* (University of New Mexico Press, 1971) describes the ways in which mail was carried over the trail before the railroad came. Studies have also begun to appear on single individuals connected with the trail, such as Larry M. Beachum's *William Becknell: Father of the Santa Fe Trade* (Texas Western Press, 1982) and Donald Chaput's *Francois X. Aubry* (Arthur H. Clark Company, 1975).

Also following the adventure book period have come guidebooks for modern travelers who wish to retrace the trail as closely as possible over today's roads. One of the first was by Margaret Long: *The Santa Fe Trail* (Denver: W. H. Kistler Company, 1954). Next came *The Road to Santa Fe* by Hobart Stocking (Hastings House, 1971). Both have been splendidly superseded by Marc Simmons's *Following the Santa Fe Trail* (Ancient City Press, 1984), recently available in an improved clothbound edition.

It is not improbable that some of the best books about the Santa Fe Trail remain to be written. Nearly everyone thought that the California-Oregon Trail had been "written out" until historian John D. Unruh, Jr., wrote his fine book *The Plains Across*, published in 1979. It showed how that trail changed through time and through the interaction between travelers and the people they encountered. To scholars, it has completely revised concepts of that trail.

The same thing could happen to the literature about the Santa Fe Trail, for so much remains hidden in manuscripts not yet published. Again, by comparison, the California-Oregon Trail has been well covered in bibliographies by Carl Wheat, Henry Wagner, Dale Morgan, and Marlin L. Heckman. Another fine bibliography, compiled by Lannon Mintz and entitled *The Trail*, will be issued this year by the University of New Mexico Press. None of these touches upon the Santa Fe Trail, and all are for collectors who need a guide to *available* materials.

The task of preparing a bibliography on *un*published materials is far more difficult, as Merrill J. Mattes can testify from his experience in compiling material on the California-Oregon Trail. It will be published this year by the University of Illinois Press under the title *Platte River Road Narratives*. Mattes knew that there were some eight hundred unpublished accounts, so he projected a probable total of 1,200; by the time he finished, several years later, he had found over 1,900 accounts and suspected that there were still more as yet unknown. To do this research, he visited forty libraries, from Yale to the Huntington, and stayed from three days to eight weeks at each. He corresponded with thirty others. Some of these libraries did not know what they had until Mattes started digging and questioning. Some had only copies and did not know whence they came. Many libraries will not permit copying; many will not allow publication; and publication of diaries, journals, and letters must be cleared with heirs. I know from past projects that this is an extremely difficult task.

But the unpublished material is out there. To give just a few examples, the Carrie Beinecke collection in the Yale library contains an 1824 Mexican government report on the Mexican attitude toward the opening of the Santa Fe Trail. The University of Missouri's Western Historical manuscript collection has a manuscript account of a trip by William Hitt over the Santa Fe Trail from St. Joseph, Missouri, to Taos around 1831. The same collection has a Mexican War manuscript journal of a doctor on the Santa Fe Trail, John Dunlap, and another such diary by Dr. Thomas Lester. The collection at the Bancroft Library is rich in manuscript material, such as Elias Brevoort's memoirs as a Santa Fe trader; Benjamin Read's collection of the papers of Manuel Alvarez, a Santa Fe merchant after 1830; Edward E. Ayer's account of a trip east over the trail in 1864; the Peter Smith papers on his experiences as a Santa Fe trader (Peter was a younger brother of Jedediah Smith); and War Department documents about the Santa Fe Trail. The Western Manuscripts collection at Utah State University in Logan, Utah, has a journal of a member of the Mormon Battalion, and many other Utah institutions have Mormon Battalion diaries. That unit traveled the trail for nearly half its length in 1846. Finally, the University of New Mexico

Library's special collections has a manuscript narrative of a Gold Rush journey over the trail in 1849. Indeed, a book needs to be written about the use of the Santa Fe Trail as a route to the gold fields—to California after 1849 and to Colorado after 1858. These are only a tip of the iceberg, but they show what wealth of untapped material is out there.

When it comes to research in newspapers, we already have a superb guide—Louise Barry's *The Beginning of the West* (Kansas State Historical Society, 1972). This massive, entertaining book gives thousands of capsule synopses of news reports, a great many about the Santa Fe Trail, up to 1854. It lists the newspaper and date, so researchers can track the item to its sources, and many of those items will be rich in detail. It is easy to see that to compile a bibliography of unpublished materials will take one person a long time, much less if there are others to help. The historical quarterlies of many historical societies should be examined, from Volume I, number 1, to the present, to locate articles about the Santa Fe Trail or people and events along the way. It is not enough to consult indexes; indexers overlook many items. The publications of local societies, such as the Westport Historical Society, or the various corrals of the Westerners need to be reviewed. State libraries must be checked. Much of this can be done by local or nearby people, especially if there is some sort of an association to steer them.

But there is much yet to be found. There is not a person interested in the Santa Fe Trail who cannot contribute to this story of a great pathway during the youth of the West.

INDEX

Abert, Lieutenant James B., 21, 61
Aguirre, Mamie Bernard, 36
Alexander, Eveline, 34, 42; comments on trail travel, 37, 41
Alphonsa, Sister Mary, 3–4
Alvarez, Manuel, 16, 79, 112
Anza, Juan Bautista de: expedition of, against Comanches, 58
Arce, Jose Maria de, 59
Arkansas Valley: settlements in, 61
Armijo, Manuel, 86; and invasion of Santa Fe, 22; land grants of, 17–18, 21, 22
Armijo, Nestor, 78
Armijo, Rafael, 81
Ashley, William, 69
Aubry, Francois X., 111
Autobees, Charles, 70
Ayer, Edward E., 114

Baca, Francisco, 78
Baca, Luis: comments on Raton Pass, 62
Bado, Salvador Martin del, 78
Baird, James, 58, 69, 70
Baird-McKnight party, 58–59, 68
Baldwin, Alice Blackwood, 34–35, 37; comments on trail travel, 39, 41, 42; gives birth on trail, 40
Beaubien, Charles (Carlos), 22, 48, 69
Becknell, William, 48, 68; crosses Raton Mountains, 59–60; establishes Cimarron Route, 60
Beckwourth, James, 70
Bent, Charles, 12, 60, 79; attitude of, toward New Mexicans, 19, 80; killed in Taos Uprising, 22; and land grants, 18, 21, 22; and Mexican authorities, 16–18; as New Mexico governor, 22, 72; and Padre Antonio José Martínez, 16–17, 18
Bent, George, 13
Bent, Robert, 13

Bent, St. Vrain & Company, 13, 60–61; dissolves, 22; origin of, 13
Bent, Silas, 12
Bent, William, 12; chastises employee, 51; offers new fort for sale, 51; and Sand Creek Massacre, 23; scouts for Kearny, 22
Benton, Thomas Hart, 54n.6
Bent's Fort, 12, 60; building of, 15; description of, 14; destroyed, 23; as headquarters for Indian agency, 72; location of, 14, 24n.4; in ruins, 52; soldiers garrisoned at, 21–22
Bent's New Fort, 51
Boggs, Thomas, 70
Boyd, Frances, 35; comments on trail travel, 40, 41
Bryan, Milt, 94–96

Cahill, Iona, 5
Carson, Kit, 71
Cather, Willa, 16
Cavallero, José, 78
Chambers, Samuel, 59, 70
Chapman, Arthur, 5
Charbonneau, Jean Baptiste, 70
Chouteau, Auguste, 59
Chouteau-DeMun party, 68
Chávez, Antonio José, 79, 96–97; murdered by McDaniel gang, 80, 97
Chávez, Mariano José, 80, 81, 90n.31
Cimarron Route (of Santa Fe Trail), 56, 60
Clay, Henry, 15
Clifford, Josephine McCrackin, 35
Collins, James L., 48
Comanche Indians: attack caravan, 95–96; cross Sangre de Cristos, 57
Connelly, Henry, 48
Cooke, Philip St. George, 81

DeMun, Jules, 59
Donnelly, Eleanor, 4

117

Doolittle, James R., 4
Dunlap, John, 114
Dye, Job, 70

Ellison, Thomas, 95
Escudero, Ramon and Manuel Simon, 78

Field, Matt, 79; describes Raton Pass in 1839, 61
Fitzpatrick, Thomas, 72
Fort Milk. *See* Pueblo de Leche
Fort St. Vrain, 15
Fort William, 70
Frémont, John Charles, 21
French traders: cross Sangre de Cristos, 57
Fur trade: rendezvous, 13; shift in pattern of, 12–13

Gantt, John, 14, 60, 72
Garrard, Lewis, 111
Gilpin, William, 22; and land grants, 20
Glenn, Hugh, 68
Gonzales, Tomás, 81
Gregg, Josiah, 48, 79, 80, 108
Gutierrez, José Mariano, 81

Harmony, Manuel X., 81
Harvey, S. B.: debunks treasure legend, 101
Harwood, Emily, 35
Hatcher, John, 70
Haxby, Lord Frederick, 3
Hitt, William, 114
Holmes, Julia Archibald, 36; comments on trail travel, 41–42
Hope, Welborn, 7
Houghton, Judge Joab, 48
Huning, Ernestine, 36, 37; comments on trail travel, 36, 40, 42

Jackson, David, 70
James, Thomas, 48

Kearny, Stephen Watts, 21–22, 98; consults with Bents, 21; crosses Raton Pass in 1846, 61
Kinkead, Mathew, 69, 71
Kirker, James, 69, 70, 72

LaTourette, Genevieve, 35
Lalande, Baptiste, 58
Lamme, Sammuel Craig, 2
Lamy, John B., 3; and death of Sister Mary Alphonsa, 3–4; fictionalized in *Death Comes for the Archbishop*, 16
Lane, Lydia Spenser, 34; comments on trail travel, 36, 39, 40
Larkin, James Ross: arrives in Santa Fe, 52; describes Bent's New Fort, 51; describes Bent's Old Fort, 51–52; diary of, 48; early life of, 48; health problems of, 49; meets Lucien Maxwell, 52; observes border conflict in Kansas, 50; and William Bent, 49, 50
Larkin, Mary Chambers, 48–49
Leese, Jacob, 69
Legends about Santa Fe Trail, 94–106
Lester, Thomas, 114
Lisa, Manuel, 59
Luna, Antonio José, 79
Lupton, Lancaster P., 70

Magoffin, Susan Shelby: comments on trail travel, 36, 38, 39, 61; journal of, 34, 111; suffers miscarriage at Bent's Fort, 40; upbringing of, 33–34
Manifest Destiny: and commercial markets, 19–20; definition of, 18–19; and election of 1844, 15–16; and industrial urbanization, 20; and land speculation, 20–21; origin of, 12, 18; and southern route to California, 21
Martinez, Jesus M., 103–4
Martínez, Padre Antonio José, 16–18, 22

Maxwell, Lucien, 52, 70
McDaniel, John, 80, 97–98; murders Antonio José Chávez, 97; trial of, 98
McKee, Anna, 35
McKnight, Robert, 59, 70
McLanahan, James, 58
Means, John, 94–95
Mendinueta, Pedro Fermin de: punitive expedition of, against Comanches, 58
Missouri Pacific Railroad, 54n.6
Mitchell, Levin, 71, 72
Morris, Anna Maria, 35; comments on trail travel, 40, 41, 42
Mountain Branch (of Santa Fe Trail), 14; earliest known reference to, 56, 63n.1

New Mexican traders, 76–81: attitudes of Anglos toward, 77–78; rise of, in 1830s, 78–79
New, Bill, 71

O'Sullivan, John: and phrase "Manifest Destiny," 18
Oliphant, Wilbur: and Lightner Ranch treasure, 103

Panic of 1837, 15
Patterson, James, 58
Pattie, James and Sylvester, 70
Pena, José Mariano de la, 78
Philibert, Joseph, 59
Pike, Zebulon Montgomery, 58, 110
Pino, Esteban, 78
Play, Jose, 49, 52
Point of Rocks, 105
Polk, James Knox, 15
Pueblo de Leche (Fort Milk), 71
Pursely, James, 58

Raton Pass, 56; conditions of, 56, 57, 61; meaning of, 65n.18
Roe, Marie Antoinette Mack, 35; comments on trail travel, 37

Rogers, James Grafton, 5
Russell, Marian Sloan, 6, 34, 62, 111
Ruxton, George F., 72
Sage, Rufus, 72
St. Vrain, Ceran, 48, 69; and land grants, 18, 21, 22
St. Vrain, Marcellin, 13–14
Sandoval, Antonio, 81
Sanford, Mrs. Byron, 35
Sangre de Cristo Pass, 56; center of travel in 1830s, 61; fortified by Governor Melgares, 59
Santa Fe Trail: compared to other overland trails, 28, 112–113; earliest known reference to, 56, 63n.1; place names of, 7–9; poetry of, 2–9
Santa Fe Trail Magazine, 4–5
Sarracino, José Rafael, 78
Sibley, George C., 48, 77
Sisters, Catholic: Sister Blandina Segale, 35; Sister Kotska Gauthreaux, 35; Sister Mary Alphonsa, 3–4; Sister Mary Joanna Welch, 35; Mother Mary Magdalen Hayden, 35
Slacum, William, 15
Smith, John, 70
Smith, Lee: and Lightner Ranch treasure, 102–3
Smith, Peter, 114
Smith, Reuben, 58
Smith, Thomas ("Peg-Leg"), 70
Spanish resistance to trade, 57, 58–59, 68
Spear, Stephen, J.: debunks treasure legend, 101
Spiegelberg, Flora, 36
Stephenson, Hugh, 48
Sublette, Andrew, 70
Sumner, Colonel E. V.: campaign of, against Cheyennes, 51

Tharp, William, 70
Trappers and Santa Fe Trail, 68–72
Trapping: and annual rendezvous, 13, 69; and decline

of beaver trade, 13, 70, 71; and
  Mexican government, 68–69;
  and whiskey trade, 69–70
Turner, Frederick Jackson, 29
Tyler, John, 15–16

Valverde y Cosio, Antonio, 57
Vigil, Donaciano, 22
Volivar, Atancio, 78

Wallace, Susan, 36; comments on
  trail travel, 38
Warfield, Charles: raids Mora,
  New Mexico, 72
Webb, James Josiah, 48
Welsh, Sister Mary Joanna:
  comments on trail travel, 37,
  38, 41, 42
Wetzel, William: and Harveyville
  hoax, 101
Williams, Ellen, 35
Wolfskill, William, 69
Women: overlooked in frontier
  history, 28–29; perceived as
  reluctant pioneers, 29–30;
  stereotypes of, in historical
  literature, 29
Women, black: on Santa Fe Trail,
  30
Women, Indian: cultural role of,
  31–32; in marriages with white
  trappers, 32; on Santa Fe Trail,
  31, 33, 50
Women, Mexican-American: and
  Anglo husbands, 33; on Santa
  Fe Trail, 32–33
Women. *See also* Sisters, Catholic
Wootton, Richens ("Uncle Dick"),
  71; builds toll road over Raton
  Pass, 62; as sheriff of Taos, 72

Yellow Woman, 50. *See also*
  Women, Indian

Yount, George C., 69

COLORADO HISTORICAL SOCIETY
BOARD OF DIRECTORS
Officers
Chair, Bruce M. Rockwell
President, Barbara Sudler
Vice-Chair, Walter A. Steele
Vice-Chair, Janis Falkenberg
Secretary, John F. Welborn
Assistant Secretary,
 James E. Hartmann
Treasurer, Roger D. Knight III
Emeritus, Stephen H. Hart

Ex-Officio Directors
The Honorable Roy R. Romer,
 Governor of Colorado
Blenda J. Wilson,
 Executive Director,
 Department of Higher
 Education
Nancy Campbell,
 President, Volunteers of
 the Society

Directors
Joan Anderman
Robert C. Black III

Curtis E. Burton
Lauren Y. Casteel
Jean S. Catherwood
Dana H. Crawford
Stanley Dempsey
William T. Eagan
Walter C. Emery
Ellen Kingman Fisher
Robert T. Herres
James P. Johnson
Frank A. Kemp
Walter A. Koelbel
Alma M. Kurtz
Liston E. Leyendecker
Carlos F. Lucero
Myron D. Neusteter
Richard T. Schlosberg III
J. Steve Sigstad
Ruth Stockton
Lydia Vandemoer
Eleanor V. Vincent
William F. Wilbur
Grant Wilkins
H. Marie Wormington

EDITORIAL REVIEW BOARD
Carl Abbott
 Portland State University
Richard A. Bartlett
 Florida State University
Maxine Benson
 Denver, Colorado
Lee Chambers-Schiller
 *University of
 Colorado-Boulder*
Vine Deloria, Jr.
 University of Arizona
David Fridtjof Halaas
 Denver, Colorado

Donald Jackson
 Colorado Springs
Oakah L. Jones
 Purdue University
Harry Kelsey
 *Los Angeles County
 Museum of Natural History*
Bruce Rippeteau
 *University of
 South Carolina*
Clark C. Spence
 *University of Illinois at
 Urbana-Champaign*